# Mending a Broken Mind

# Mending a Broken Mind

*Healing the Whole Person Who Suffers with Clinical Depression*

ANDREW ADAM WHITE, MD

*Foreword by Frank Dennehy, MD*

CASCADE *Books* • Eugene, Oregon

MENDING A BROKEN MIND
Healing the Whole Person Who Suffers with Clinical Depression

Cascade Books
An Imprint of Wipf and Stock Publishers
199 W. 8th Ave., Suite 3
Eugene, OR 97401

www.wipfandstock.com

PAPERBACK ISBN: 978-1-7252-8802-7
HARDCOVER ISBN: 978-1-7252-8803-4
EBOOK ISBN: 978-1-7252-8804-1

*Cataloguing-in-Publication data:*

Names: White, Andrew Adam, MD; foreword, Frank Dennehy, MD.

Title: Mending a broken mind : healing the whole person who suffers with clinical depression / Andrew Adam White, MD ; foreword by Frank Dennehy, MD.

Description: Eugene, OR: Cascade Books, 2021 | Includes bibliographical references.

Identifiers: ISBN 978-1-7252-8802-7 (paperback) | ISBN 978-1-7252-8803-4 (hardcover) | ISBN 978-1-7252-8804-1 (ebook)

Subjects: LCSH: Depression, Mental. | Depression—Mental—Religious aspects, Christianity. | Depressed persons—Religious life.

Classification: BV4910.34 .W50 2021 (paperback) | BV4910.34 (ebook)

09/02/21

To my dear wife, Fenni,
and all those who care for those suffering from depression.

# Contents

# Foreword

YOU HOLD A TREASURE in your hands, because of what it is and for whom it is written. A book like this has been a long time in coming. Dr. White's book represents over a century of development in modern medicine and psychology. In the late 1800s, medicine began to separate the spiritual side of human experience from the purely physical and observed side. Dr. White brings back together the body, mind, and important spiritual aspects of who we are. He writes for a very broad audience, and includes real-life stories of suffering and recovery.

Dr. Sigmund Freud had a huge impact on medicine and psychology in the early 1900s. He was an astute observer of behavior, but his atheistic bias as one of the founders of modern psychiatry led him to numerous faulty conclusions. He and other leaders cemented the notion in Western medicine that God and religion must be separated from medical science. Since then, many physicians over the years have been ostracized for reporting on observations that show elements of faith and its effect. Dr. Alexis Carrel was a 1912 Nobel prize-winning physician in France. Because he was a firsthand witness to a miraculous cure of terminal tuberculosis at the Lourdes shrine in France, he lost his standing on the faculty of medicine in Lyons. Fast forward eight decades and the bias continued against exploring spiritual dimensions and medicine. In the 1980s, Dr. Randolph Byrd did the first large randomized, controlled, double-blinded study of the effect of intercessory prayer on critically ill patients in an intensive care unit. Despite the strong study design, and because of the significant positive findings, he had great difficulty in getting his results published. Since that time, however, numerous additional and larger studies have shown the same positive effects of prayer on medical outcomes, even when patients did not know they were being prayed for, or had no faith themselves. The modern world of Christian psychology in the last thirty to forty years has made tremendous leaps in understanding and success in treatment. This success results from what Pope John Paul II called a "Christian anthropology." By bringing God and a patient's faith back into the picture, we are allowed a deeper understanding of who we really are in our entirety. Such a deeper understanding helps to reveal the underlying sources and meaning of our suffering, as well as how best to relieve it. However, physicians still face scorn when reporting on or including elements of a patient's faith. Dr. White shows courage in writing this book.

Who will benefit from this book? First, patients who have suffered a deep depression, and their family and friends. Giving hope are the real-life stories of real people moving from suffering to recovery. Here are plain language explanations of what depression is and how it can be treated. Medicines, counseling methods, and other helps are laid out for easy understanding. Patients of Christian faith will begin to understand the powerful role this faith plays in successful recovery, and find meaning in the suffering while it is ongoing. Some Christians do not seek help for the symptoms of depression, fearing that depression is from weakness or personal defect or lack of faith. This book will show you how to seek help and why. For family and friends, the very real and practical ways to effectively aid and listen to a suffering depressed patient will be valuable in walking along the journey with a loved one.

Second, pastors will find this book useful in understanding those who come to them for help, as well as the basics of screening and counseling techniques that can be effective in their work. The medical sections will help guide referral for those under their care, if needed.

Third, psychology and counseling students will find a useful summary of the biology of depression and its medical treatments, and practical details of the counseling techniques that they will use in the care of patients. The religion sections cover the place and power of a patient's religious faith, and how working with this faith can assist recovery.

Finally, medical students and primary care physicians will find a helpful review of the diagnostic methods and treatment options to help patients, as well as how the patient's faith may aid in healing. The medical treatments will be familiar, but most physicians will learn some details beyond their own training. Many of the screening techniques, but not all, will also be familiar, and presented in a very practical way. The review of counseling methods is clear and concise, and serves as a good guide for use and referral. This review is not easily found elsewhere in medical training.

Who wrote this book? Andrew White, MD, is a very sharp family physician, healer, and educator. I have always admired his medical knowledge and his skill with patients. As a family physician in practice, I came to my own medical teaching role many years ago, because I was drawn to his vision for family medicine and the impact of faith on healing. Our discussions over the years have included our own walks of religious faith. Dr. White is a Christian who has suffered mightily. I have witnessed some of this suffering and disability, and I have rejoiced with him on his journey of recovery. He is an expert on depression from both sides: sufferer and healer. He has been a devout and knowledgeable Christian throughout. He is a graduate of one of the best seminaries in the country, with a strong and sound foundation in biblical understanding.

So, whether you are a sufferer yourself, family or friend, or a medical practitioner, I recommend to you this well-done work on healing a broken mind.

Frank Dennehy, MD, FAAFP
Family Physician and Residency Program Director
Virginia
August 2020

# Getting Started

DEPRESSION, A TERRIBLY DISTRESSING and often disabling illness, is very common. In a 2019 survey, the National Institute of Mental Health (NIMH) found that 7.1 percent of Americans were currently suffering from major depression. Major depression was defined as: "A period of at least two weeks when a person experienced a depressed mood or loss of interest or pleasure in daily activities, and had a majority of specified symptoms, such as problems with sleep, eating, energy, concentration, or self-worth."

The NIMH also found that the prevalence of depression is 13.3 percent among adolescents aged twelve to seventeen and 13.1 percent in young adults, aged eighteen to twenty-five. Depression is the leading cause of disability in the United States and worldwide. These statistics were generated before the COVID pandemic and I believe the percentage has significantly increased since then. The World Health Organization says the statistics worldwide have doubled since the pandemic. You may be one many of those plagued with depression. If not, you probably know people suffering from it, whether you recognize it in them or not.

I've written this book primarily for those of you who suffer from depression and those who care about you. I hope that this book will help you better understand depression and give you hope for healing. I have tried to make it readable for most depressed people. Some of you, who have too much trouble with concentration or too little motivation to do almost anything, may need a caring companion to read this book and share relevant material with you a little bit at a time.

This book is secondarily written for Christians in the healing professions. Pastors and priests, Christian counselors, and Christian healthcare providers may want to recommend this book to people with clinical depression, or to their families and friends. This book looks at depression from three perspectives: the medical (including the psychiatric), the counseling, and the pastoral care perspective. If you, as a Christian healer, have not looked into all three aspects of depression, this book may increase your effectiveness in helping depressed people. For example, a pastor or priest or Christian counselor might want more information on the diagnostic tools and treatment options available to physicians and other healthcare providers. A clergyperson or Christian primary care healthcare provider may benefit from a basic understanding of commonly used professional counseling techniques, such as cognitive behavioral therapy and interpersonal therapy. Christian counselors, clergy, and healthcare providers may want more biblical insight into understanding and treating depression.

In this book, I focus specifically on clinical depression. Although "clinical depression" is not the best medical terminology, I think it conveys to lay people the difference between mild depression and more severe depression. In the medical literature, major depression is the most common terminology and it is generally categorized as mild, moderate, moderately severe, and severe. In this book I address issues most relevant to moderate and especially moderately severe and severe depression. I've read many books and articles in which authors address all levels of severity, from low-grade discouragement to severe depression. But I believe that moderate and especially moderately severe to severe depression is significantly different from discouragement and mild depression. Moderately to severely depressed people need to be cared for and treated differently. Many of the challenges Christian healers would pose to a mildly depressed person might shatter a fragile, more severely depressed person who tries, often unsuccessfully, to meet those challenges, thereby becoming even more discouraged.

I write from my head and from my heart. My writing has been strongly influenced by my personal struggles with recurrent clinical depression (seven depressions—completely disabling in two cases), my experience as a Christian family physician caring for thousands of depressed patients, teaching on depression to family medicine resident physicians in the United States and Kenya, and leading a depression support group. I have also gleaned helpful insights from the vast knowledge base on depression now available in the medical (including psychiatric), counseling, and pastoral care literature. I will also share what I have learned from the Bible, with help from trustworthy commentaries, Christian authors, and seminary professors.

Many recent Christian books on depression use the metaphor of "dark" or "darkness" in their titles: *When the Darkness Will Not Lift; Looking Up from the Stubborn Darkness; When Life Goes Dark; Light in the Darkness;* and *Darkness is My Only Companion.* This metaphor is a good one because it recognizes the "darkness-like" mood present in a large majority of people suffering from moderate to severe depression. But there are many other functions of the mind that are broken in depression, not just the mood. Your brain may not be able to sleep soundly or for long, and insomnia can be a torment. Your broken will may be so incapacitated that you are unable to be decisive in making good choices for healing, or your broken will may no longer motivate you to complete even a few essential tasks. You may feel overwhelming fatigue with an intense loss of physical as well as mental energy. These are just a few of the things broken in the mind of a clinically depressed person.

This book is titled *Mending a Broken Mind*, because it addresses many of the symptoms of a mind broken by depression, not only a dark mood. My only reservation with the title is that the word *mending* at first conjures up memories of my mother effortlessly sewing up a pant leg torn climbing a tree or my wife quickly supergluing a figurine I accidentally broke, with the crack barely visible. Clinical depression is definitely not that straightforward or that easy to mend. Healing from clinical depression is not like ordering online from Amazon.com and receiving what you have ordered in a couple of days. At best, those with clinical depression will begin to be healed two to four weeks after starting an antidepressant and/or counseling regimen. For many others it will take months, even years.

For any number of reasons, many people with depression will not seek medical, counseling, or Christian spiritual help. Why? Some people may not know what depression is with its varying modes of presentation and varying levels of severity. Some people are afraid they will be stigmatized by their depression. In fact, in some circles, it still is a somewhat stigmatized illness. Some depressed people live in denial; admitting their depressive symptoms would make them feel more vulnerable. Newly depressed people who have always thought of themselves as being "strong" may have trouble facing a real weakness of the mind, not a weakness of character. Some people feel embarrassed by their depression. In fact, embarrassment can be another face of shame that is common in depression. Some people believe that to be depressed is a sin or the result of a sin, maybe even a divine punishment. Some people feel so hopeless they think treatment will not help. Ask yourself, what do I not want So-and-So to know about me? Addressing this question may help you determine what is keeping you from getting help. If you are one of the many people who have not sought help for your depression, this book will be a good place for you to start your search for healing.

This book is not intended to deal with depression comprehensively but to motivate readers to look into medical (including psychiatric) treatment, counseling, and pastoral care. If you have already started your search, I hope this book will deepen your understanding of depression and increase your knowledge of viable roads to healing.

I write from a Christian perspective. God has been careful to make sure that those who wrote the books of the Bible declared his Word, not just their own, through the inspiration of the Holy Spirit. Subsequent generations affirmed that each of the Bible's books was truly a part of God's Word in the canonization process, again through the inspiration of the Holy Spirit. That being said, I do not believe, like some Christians, that the Bible fully addresses every troubling issue that we encounter in our lives. I believe that everyone can discover from the Bible what is necessary for faith and salvation. I also believe that no true knowledge deviates from clear biblical teaching. However, in understanding depression and effective treatments for it, we can pluck the many fruits of common-grace knowledge from neurobiology, medicine, psychology, and sociology alongside the special-grace knowledge found in the Bible, including the meaning and relevance of the birth, life, death, resurrection, and teachings of Jesus Christ.

This book is especially written for clinically depressed Christians who have a Christian worldview. I am not trying to be exclusive—the gospel is not exclusive. I just realize that many non-Christians are not interested in the Christian perspective on anything. If you are not a Christian, you can ignore the specifically Christian aspects of this book that you may find at best irrelevant or at worst offensive. Many non-Christians, even some Christians, believe you should keep your faith private. I do not. I also believe that if you are seeking God, you will see how helpful the Bible and the Christian faith is in addressing the very common human condition of depression.

I have tried to seriously address some of the most important biomedical and psychosocial aspects of depression. In these areas, I share a lot of common ground with unbelievers. But I also aim to be guided by Scripture with the aid of the Holy Spirit. Of course, I have a professional and ethical responsibility to respect all religions. I am happy, however, to share relevant Christian beliefs with unbelievers if they want to hear them. Because I trust in God's work in depressed people's lives independent from my counsel, in my medical practice I am willing to treat depression without addressing the Christian spiritual aspects. When obese diabetics come to me for care, I share with them how important it is to lose weight through diet and exercise. But if they don't lose weight, and many do not, I don't withhold important medicines to bring down their blood glucose. The goal is to get their blood glucoses down by any and all means.

I have tried to keep this book relatively short without ignoring the most helpful information—short because I recognize how hard it is for clinically depressed people to concentrate and become motivated. For the same reason, I have also not included footnotes. The lack of footnotes, however, should not be interpreted as minimizing my dependence on the writings and teachings of other knowledgeable people. Very little of what I have written is original. At the end of my book, I have included a selected bibliography of some of the resources that helped me most, those that did not help me at all, or, worse, some that I deemed hurtful.

My passion for writing on depression came after a miraculous healing from metastatic kidney cancer five years ago. That healing was also the beginning of healing from the longest and last of my seven depressions. I start my book with a summary of my own story, in hopes that it will be of help to you in your journey toward healing.

# Acknowledgments

FIRST AND FOREMOST, I am thankful for my wife, Fenni, whose steadfast love for me never waned during my depressions. She was a source of comfort in my worst moments, which were often. Laurelle Moody's prayers add so much to this book. When I read them, I feel like I am praying with her. I envy her prayer life. The courage it took for Stuart, Candace, and Brenda to share their stories of depression is no small thing. All three are so transparent and each story is beautifully written. Rev. Ken Nydam, a former pastor and current Christian counselor in Michigan, reviewed my book early in the editing process and shared with me many new insights, especially in counseling and Christian spiritual guidance. His confidence that the book would be an important contribution was very encouraging. Dr. Gordon Hugenberger is a dear Christian friend, Old Testament biblical scholar, and mentor in scriptural interpretation and its application. His insights into some of the spiritual helps and myths made them much better. Gordon has encouraged me for many years to write this book. Dr. Frank Dennehy is also a dear Christian friend and is a medical colleague. His positive comments in the foreword of the book are very gracious—far beyond my imagination. My psychiatrist, Dr. Robert Lizer, never gave up on me during the more than twenty years that I have been his patient. There are too many people to list who supported and prayed for me during my most recent depression, but here are some of them: Susan Ellwell and Dr. Robert Wesche have prayed for me almost every day for most of my professional life. I just can't imagine that commitment to intercessory prayer. There is also Dr. Eli Snelgrove, Rev. Jeff Moody, Rev. Daryl Fenton, Bruce Duerson, Rev. Patrick Ware, Meta Scott, Dr. Mike Chupp, Dr. Greg and Dorinda Beale, Rod DeArment, the Israels, the Raes, my siblings, and my children. Evelyn Bence did a wonderful job with the first professional editing. Breaking into the book publishing market is no small thing for a new author, and Rodney Clapp facilitated that. I am in his debt along with some of his colleagues at Wipf and Stock Publishers.

# *About the Author*

DR. ANDREW WHITE PRACTICES family medicine in Winchester, Virginia. He has taught on mental illness, especially depression, for more than twenty-five years. He is an Associate Clinical Professor of Family Medicine at Virginia Commonwealth University and was the founding director of the Shenandoah Valley Family Medicine Residency. Dr. White holds a Master of Arts degree in Theological Studies from Gordon-Conwell Theological Seminary. He is a Lay Eucharistic Minister in the Anglican Church in North America. He has a dear wife, Fenni, of forty-three years, and four loving children—Aaron, Joshua, Grace, and Micah.

# 1

## *My Story of Recurrent Depression*

THERE ARE COMMON THEMES that run through all depressed people's stories, and yet every person's journey is unique. Sometimes there are small variations in our stories and sometimes the chasms seem wide. Just telling your own story of depression and listening to others' can open a closed gate, through which you can walk toward healing. So here is mine.

I have struggled on and off with depression since age eleven. My father was a medical missionary to the Belgian Congo (now the Democratic Republic of Congo). My mother homeschooled the three older siblings including me, the eldest. When I was about to enter the fifth grade, my mother no longer felt adequate to teach me. I traveled about three hours from home and entered a boarding school in the capital of the Congo, Leopoldville (now Kinshasa). After school each day for the first few months, I would climb up into the attic of my new home and cry until I lay spent and exhausted. The hosting family tried to include me in their daily lives, but they were not my family. This may have just been homesickness; if so, it was extraordinarily severe and prolonged. In one letter home, I asked my mother to send me a picture of the family because I was forgetting what everyone looked like. I was heartbroken and felt abandoned.

## YOUTHFUL DESPAIR

At the age of fourteen, when I lived in Marquette, Michigan, I took one puff of hashish (my first and only experimentation with illicit drugs), which triggered a panic attack that led to a severe depression. Because it was precipitated by drug use, I was afraid to tell anyone about it and so suffered alone for the six months it took me to recover.

For me, depression is not just the usual depressed mood, loss of interest in pleasurable activities, low energy . . . which is bad enough. For me, depression is hopeless despair, searing mental agony, extreme anxiety and agitation, paralyzing helplessness, and a disabling inability to concentrate and remember things.

I was nineteen years old when I started medical school at the University of Michigan in 1973. Toward the end of my first two demanding years, I slowly slipped into a mild depression. The week after finishing my second year, I suffered a panic attack that triggered a depression so severe and so prolonged that I had to take a year-long leave of absence. I had been scheduled to do a medical student summer clerkship at Massachusetts General Hospital. Though I was frightened to go, my parents thought it might snap me out of my nervous breakdown (that is what clinical depression was often called back then). During the first three days at Mass General, I felt as if I was in a house of horrors, terrified almost every moment of the day. A mental wreck, I resigned and took a same-day flight back home.

I was unable to study medicine or work because of concentration and memory problems, in addition to the mental agony. I did almost nothing except ruminate about depressing and terrorizing things. My mother says that during that time I would sit for hours with my Bible open in my lap, wet with tears from crying out to God for healing. Jesus had healed so many people, why wouldn't he heal me? I would not even turn the page of my Bible because I could hardly read a sentence or two.

Several different psychotropic drug regimens were ineffective (there weren't many antidepressants in those days). Psychological and spiritual counseling resulted in no improvement. In deep, hopeless despair from the torment of the depression, I attempted suicide. I had a loaded handgun pointed to my temple but could not pull the trigger. I did, however, take a lethal overdose of a sedative that I found in the medicine closet of our house (remember, my father was a physician). As the sedative took effect, I noticed a slight improvement in my mental agony and terror, which gave me a sliver of hope that I might be healed. I told my younger brother what I had done and was soon in the emergency room. After three days in the intensive care unit, I was given electroconvulsive therapy (ECT), commonly known as electric shock therapy. On the fourth treatment, I suddenly, dramatically improved. I was placed on an antidepressant and mood stabilizer to reinforce the healing from ECT. The anxiety and panic attacks, however, continued for some time, due, in part, to my great fear of a relapse. Fortunately, I was able to return to my medical studies later that year. After a year, my medications were discontinued. It wasn't known back then that recurrent or especially severe depression needs to be treated for life.

When I completed medical school at the age of twenty-four in 1978, my new bride, Fenni, and I moved to Charleston, South Carolina, where I started a three-year combined internship and residency in family medicine (then called family practice). During the orientation before starting my internship, I rapidly developed another severe depression. I thought I would have to delay my internship, but fortunately the medication I was prescribed kicked in fairly quickly. I didn't miss any days of my internship though I was very distressed for several months. Again, after a year my medications were discontinued.


## MISSION MADNESS

In my second year of family medicine residency training, I went on a medical mission trip to the Thailand side of the Thailand-Cambodian border during the refugee crisis precipitated by the Communist Khmer Rouge (Cambodian Red) genocide. A Vietnamese offensive into Cambodia in the early spring of 1979 violently pushed the Khmer Rouge, along with many of the terrorized civilians they controlled, over the Thailand border. One of the Khmer Rouge-dominated refugee camps was Sa Kaeo. There were other refugee camps that housed some Cambodian military who opposed the Khmer Rouge, along with civilian followers. They were all escaping from the truly evil Khmer Rouge and from the greatly feared but, in retrospect, much less evil Vietnamese.

Early in the spring of 1980 at our church, Fenni and I heard about the terrible conditions on the Thailand border. On the way home that Sunday, on the radio we heard more about this humanitarian crisis. I immediately felt called to go help, but we both knew there were no opportunities for mission service until I graduated from my residency program. But then, that very next day, I found in my residency mailbox a letter from the dean of the medical school. The dean encouraged us young doctors to consider going to the Thailand-Cambodian border with all costs paid by the Southern Baptist Convention and with residency training credit given. Within a week after the dean's letter, three of my extended family members wrote, saying they had heard of the crisis and wondered if there was some way I could go to

Southeast Asia. None of the three was aware of what had just transpired in my life. It seemed obvious that God was calling me to go to the Thailand-Cambodian border, so I signed up. Our mission team was comprised of seven resident physicians and one faculty physician. For several weeks, we met regularly to bond together and prepare for the mission trip.

When I stepped off the plane in Thailand, I had a panic attack that triggered yet another severe depression. Despite my condition, God used me as a leader in a Christian revival among some of the vilest people in the history of the world, the Khmer Rouge. In terms of percentage of the population murdered violently or by forced labor and starvation along with the fatal diseases that accompany starvation, the Khmer Rouge were the worst in modern history; this genocide was every bit as horrible as the Jewish Holocaust. (For more on this genocide see the movie *The Killing Fields* and/ or read the book *Intended for Evil*.)

I was initially assigned to a mission hospital in Thailand to help me understand Thai culture and local medical practice. Fortunately, I surreptitiously found some imipramine (an antidepressant that had helped me in the past) in the hospital pharmacy. Unfortunately, it takes four to six weeks for the antidepressant to really begin to take effect.

Two weeks later, I was stationed along at a non-Khmer Rouge military and civilian refugee camp. Because there was such an outpouring of medical humanitarian aid, there was almost nothing for our team to do. Of course, I could not understand why God had given me such a clear calling to what seemed to be a useless mission. Not only that, but I was reeling from being away from the support and security of my wife, still at home. After two weeks, a request came from Sa Kaeo, one of the hated Khmer Rouge-dominated refugee camps. The request was for a physician to serve in the place of a physician who had become ill.

Now the worst thing depressed people can do, from a psychological perspective, is to leave their support groups. I knew this, but I also felt the same clear call from God that I had felt when I originally signed up for the mission. My calling to Sa Kaeo was confirmed when none of the other team members were willing to go. Of course, I had to quickly overcome my abhorrence of the Khmer Rouge, which was no small thing.

Thankfully my medical responsibilities at the Sa Kaeo camp did not require much concentration—concentration that was severely lacking because of my depression. I ran a tent hospital malaria ward with about fifty patients; thankfully almost everyone needed the same treatment so my concentration was not an issue. My seemingly more important though small role was in the Christian revival, which started on my hospital ward, that miraculously took place at Sa Kaeo. The first day, the patients assigned to my ward (Khmer

Rouge military and civilians alike) were too ill for me to share the gospel with them. On the second day, most had improved medically and could understand what I was saying. I simply asked each patient through an interpreter, "Do you know you are a sinner?" One hundred percent said yes. Can you imagine that response in the modern Western world? Then I told each one of them, "Tomorrow I will bring you good news." Those fourteen words were literally all I could manage to say—being so severely depressed. Amazingly, approximately one-quarter of the patients on my ward couldn't wait until the next day to hear the good news. They went to our hospital ward chaplain and, upon hearing the good news, started a new life in Jesus. The chaplain had been a missionary in Cambodia before he retired. Though he had not had a very fruitful ministry, he had translated the New Testament Gospel of John into a Cambodian dialect understood by the refugees at Sa Kaeo.

On the third day, the one-quarter of my patients who had met with the chaplain had big smiles on their faces, eager to share with me their newfound faith. To the remaining three-quarters, I shared the gospel of salvation by faith in Jesus Christ that would cleanse one from all sin no matter how terrible. This time God gave me a few (but not many) more words regarding God's grace to share with my patients. Another one-quarter immediately accepted the good news and began a life-transforming relationship with Jesus. I directed them, of course, to the hospital ward chaplain to ground them in their newfound faith.

One of the Khmer Rouge leaders with malaria experienced a spiritual rebirth. He would often read aloud from the book of John, which the chaplain had translated, to the entire ward. This reading was miraculous, because the Khmer Rouge had routinely killed anyone who could read. Those who were literate were perceived to be an intellectual threat to the Khmer Rouge Communist ideology.

God also raised up a Cambodian evangelist. He had been a believer for only three weeks, but he was daily discipled by our hospital ward chaplain. This evangelist went from home church to home church (more accurately home shack church to home shack church) sharing the gospel from sunrise to sunset. His life was in great danger. Some of the Khmer Rouge leaders had told the people that they would have to "sleep on the ground" if they converted to Christianity. This was a euphemism for digging your own grave. Probably from a combination of fear and mental exhaustion, this evangelist would come to my ward each night physically shaking and unable to sleep. He needed a shot of a tranquilizer (Valium) to calm down and get some much-needed rest.

Four improbable vessels were the leaders of this miraculous Sa Kaeo revival: (1) a severely depressed family physician resident who could hardly speak, (2) a retired missionary minister to Cambodia who had seen little fruit in his ministry there but was our hospital ward chaplain, (3) a miraculously alive Khmer Rouge leader who regularly read aloud from the Gospel of John given to him by its translator, our hospital ward chaplain, and (4) a newly converted Cambodian evangelist who was mentally exhausted and afraid for his life. I later heard that when the Sa Kaeo revival had run its God-ordained course, two to three thousand people in the camp had come into a personal relationship with Jesus Christ.

At the time of this miraculous revival, I experienced no joy because of the severity of my depression. God apparently did not need my joy to bring about the revival. But today I am filled with great joy every time I remember God's work at Sa Kaeo. I have come to believe that God chose me and the other leaders of this revival because of our weaknesses so that he would get all the glory. When Paul was suffering from "a thorn [that] was given me in the flesh," the Lord said to him, "My grace is sufficient for you, for my power is made perfect in weakness" (2 Corinthians 12:7, 9). The Lord certainly made his power perfect in the weakness of my severe depression.

## MIDDLE-AGE EPISODES

At the age of forty-four, in 1997, I had yet another depression just before starting a demanding job as founding director of a new family medicine residency in Winchester and Front Royal, Virginia—the Shenandoah Valley Family Medicine Residency. For the first few months, I was almost completely incapacitated, but my supervisor encouraged me to endure for the sake of the residency. Fortunately, my secretary supported me during this time when I was partially disabled by keeping me from being overwhelmed with the work of starting a residency. I fully recovered over the next few months, in large part because of being prescribed an antidepressant, and greatly enjoyed the next seven years in my position as residency director.

Seven years after starting the residency, which was in 2004, I needed to step down from my position as residency director. I enjoyed the creative aspect of starting a residency and the teaching, but I did not enjoy the day-to-day administration, including personnel issues, and consequently was not good at it. Coming to recognize my weakness in leading the residency was a blow to my self-esteem. Only two of my medical colleagues at the residency or associated with the residency supported me during my difficult transition back into private practice—another severe blow. I felt disgraced and deeply ashamed for years. My colleagues seemed to remember only my very real failures and none of my few but important successes. Dr. Eli

Snelgrove was my strongest advocate for joining the practice with which he was associated. Stepping down as residency director and entering private practice was stressful enough to trigger yet another depression. Fortunately, a very effective new residency director, Dr. Frank Dennehy, played a leading role in helping the residency not only survive but thrive even to this day. Frank met with me every few months after I left, and I don't know how to put in words what a moral support he was to me. He reassured me that I had gotten the residency off to a good start—affirmation that my shattered self-image really needed (in truth some parts of my self-image needed to be broken). At the onset of this depression, I was already on an antidepressant. At first, this depression was mild, but it very slowly worsened over many years, until it became as severe as my worst previous depression, in medical school, and it was much longer than any of the others—over ten years long. Almost every month, my psychiatrist tried a new antidepressant or mood stabilizer or a stronger dose of either without effect.

By 2013, when I was fifty-nine years old, I was so depressed that I could no longer work. My concentration and memory were so severely affected that I could not practice medicine. I would go into one of my examination rooms, take a history from the patient, and perform a physical exam. When I stepped out to record my notes, I could remember almost nothing from the patient encounter. I was no longer mentally competent in my role as a family physician. The inevitable necessity of giving up patient care added to my already severe depression, since I have always greatly loved the practice of medicine. When I was about two-and-one-half years old, I was given a dime from a neighbor who suggested I buy a box of Cracker Jacks when I was with my mother at the grocery store. I, however, promptly put on one of my father's surgical caps and a surgical mask and walked to the local dime store alone. When I went to the counter with my Cracker Jacks, I was asked who I was. I told the clerk I was Dr. White. I can never remember a time when I didn't want to become a doctor, so I was devastated when I was unable to practice medical science and art.

In my disabled condition, I was in great mental torment. Almost nothing brought me any relief. Singing with others at church and taking part in the Anglican liturgy, including the Eucharist, gave me a short-lived, partial reprieve. My pastor, Patrick Ware, spent an hour every week for many months listening to me and comforting me in a coffee shop, giving me short-lived, partial reprieves from mental pain. At first, I could build models and do puzzles. I took a stained-glass course and actually made a few beautiful pieces. I could play games with an elementary-school boy as a Big Brother and stock shelves at a volunteer-run food pantry. For a while I was a local hospice volunteer. Often the dying only needed a few words of comfort or just my silent presence. Later I could only do weeding at a public garden. For several hours a day, I would kneel on brick-paved trails and pull out weeds, one by one, between the bricks. Finally, all I could do was lie in my bed or sit in my easy chair day after day, doing absolutely nothing except enduring mental agony. Sleep was a mixed blessing. Falling asleep was a great relief, but awakening was terror upon terror.

## I PLANNED MY FUNERAL

Two years later, in 2015 when I was sixty-one, after two terrible years of unemployment and mental misery, I suddenly developed shortness of breath. The physician assistant who examined me ordered a CT scan of the chest looking for blood clots. Although my lungs were normal, the scan included images low enough to detect a large kidney cancer with metastases to the lymph nodes in my abdomen and chest. I was actually relieved when I received the news that I had metastatic kidney cancer. God was taking me home. I had been depressed for so long and so severely that I wanted to die. One of my very caring brothers encouraged everyone to pray that I would be healed from both cancer and depression—or neither. If I were not to be cured from the unbearable mental pain of depression, my family, like me, did not want me to be cured from cancer.

I went on a farewell cruise to Alaska with my daughter, who wanted some time alone with her father before he died. She was troubled by the fact that I did not want to live. I planned my funeral with my brother-in-law, an Episcopal priest who loves Jesus. I bought a tombstone; the epitaph reads "Though he slay me, yet will I hope in him," which is from Job 13:15, KJV. Job, we will soon see, suffered a severe depression. Whereas I was suicidal in my medical school depression, which was as severe as this one, I could now put my trust in a God who loved me even though it didn't feel as if he loved me at all. Because I strongly believe in the power of healing prayer, I was publicly prayed for and anointed with oil. After that, virtually all my fellow congregants and many from churches all over the world regularly prayed for me.

ANDREW ADAM
*BELOVED*
1953

THOUGH HE SLAY ME,
YET WILL I HOPE IN HIM

## ONE AND THREE-FOURTHS MIRACLES

Just prior to kidney cancer surgery, I underwent a preoperative MRI and an even more sensitive PET scan. There was no longer any evidence of cancer metastases to the lymph nodes, even though I had not undergone chemotherapy or immunotherapy or any other treatment. In surgery, the kidney cancer was found to be four-and-one-half pounds. The cancerous kidney and the surrounding lymph nodes were removed. The pathology report indicated that the cancer was contained within the kidney capsule and that all twenty-three lymph nodes removed in surgery showed no signs of cancer. I could not stop privately and publicly praising God for his supernatural intervention in my life. My oncologist said it was not possible for me to have been healed from my cancer without other treatment. A medical colleague said the enlarged lymph nodes must have been due to some other condition that had resolved, which is possible but not probable. It is hard for people who do not believe in supernatural healing to recognize a supernatural healing when it is the most likely reason for the healing.

Simultaneously, on the day of surgery, my depression began to lift. I had been on scores of different antidepressants and mood stabilizers, but none of them worked well or for long. I had also had two series of electroconvulsive therapy and two series of transcranial magnetic stimulation. The first of each series helped a little but not the second. The night before my kidney cancer surgery, a psychiatry resident physician at the National Institutes of Health ordered a small dose of a psychotropic medicine to help me sleep. I had previously been on two very similar medicines for depression without any remediation at all. I slept well, and in the morning, I felt just the slightest bit of a lifting of my depression. When my regular psychiatrist heard this, he steadily increased the dose of the medication until it was forty times the original dose. This was the beginning of the end of a horrible chapter in my life history. One year later in 2016, when I was sixty-two years old, I returned to half-time practice of medicine, and I have never been more content and satisfied in my professional and personal life. Because of my mental fragility, I really cannot do medical work more than half time, but I can think, read, pray, teach, and write.

I think of these healings as one and three-fourths miracles. The healing from metastatic cancer seems to me to be a genuine, full-fledged miracle. My healing from depression is not a miracle in a strict sense, since it started with a psychotropic medication change. However, the timing of the beginning of my healing from depression to the very same day as curative kidney cancer surgery seems more than a coincidence to me.

I am not sure why Jesus heals some people and not others, but I think I know part of the reason in my case. And it was *not* because I was sinless and had great faith. There were many ways God wanted my life to change before taking me to his home. Here are some of the beneficial changes I see in my life as result of my depression and my healing from depression:

1.  An improved devotional life in terms of quality and quantity—including (1) scholarly and meditative study of the Bible, (2) reflection on the words of Christian authors from the early church to the present, and (3) intercessory prayer. My relationship with Jesus has never been closer.

2.  More involvement in the lives of others, especially Christian men who like me need regular time to share with each other.

3.  More involvement in my church as a lay eucharistic minister, in its healing prayer ministry, and teaching on the Bible, especially from the Old Testament.

4.  Teaching and writing more on mental illness, especially depression.

There are many specific ways that experiencing depression and being healed from it changed my life, but here I note just one. As a lay eucharistic minister, I'm honored to share the chalice of wine with fellow believers every week. I say, "This is the blood of Christ which was shed for you." Before my last depression, my memory for names was pitifully poor and then it worsened. Since I was healed, including healing from memory loss, I have trained myself to remember the names of all the people who regularly attend our church's early service. Remembering names of those who come forward for the bread and the wine now comes easily to me. I love personalizing the administration of the wine. "Alberto, this is the blood of Christ which was shed for *you*." "Laura, this is the blood of Christ which was shed for *you*."

For years I had taught on mental illness to US medical students and family medicine residents, but now I felt called to greatly expand my efforts, teaching especially on depression and anxiety. I teach in my home, in our community, and in churches in Virginia and abroad in Kenya, especially at Tenwek Hospital. At Tenwek, I teach Kenyan interns and family medicine residents, clinical officers (akin to American physician assistants), nursing students, community health workers, hospital chaplains, and chaplain students. I teach on mental illness using insights from medicine, counseling, and the Christian faith.

I had started a master of arts in theological studies at Gordon-Conwell Theological Seminary in 1983, when I was thirty years old. I had been in full-time family practice for two years and reduced my practice to two-thirds time, allowing me to complete a two-year degree in six years. Since seminary training, I have had a love for the Old Testament. In the past, my study of Scripture was for my own edification, which is a good enough reason to study the Bible. But since recovering from my last depression, I taught on the Old Testament on a blog site for one year. I also teach it in person to Kenyan chaplain students at Tenwek Hospital. A proficient knowledge of the Old Testament really helps Christians better understand (1) God's nature and acts throughout human history, (2) Jesus' person and ministry for the last three of his years of his earthly life, (3) the ongoing power and work of the Holy Spirit, and (4) the mission of the church, the new, expanding Israel. I have found the Old Testament to be particularly helpful in teaching on mental illness.

I enjoy caring for patients with depression and my personal experience with depression is not the only reason why. When I make the diagnosis of diabetes, most patients don't have symptoms, or they might have only mild symptoms, such as increased thirst, frequent urination, and blurred vision. When I treat them, their blood sugars come down as the result of major lifestyle changes, appropriate medication management, and regular blood sugar monitoring. These changes help prevent future permanent nerve damage, blindness, and kidney failure from prolonged high blood sugars. Newer diabetes medications also help prevent future heart attacks, strokes, and leg and foot amputations. Despite the improvement in their blood sugars and a decreased risk of serious complications in the future, when these newly diagnosed diabetics see me for follow-up, they rarely claim that their lives are better. In fact, their lives are more complicated, difficult, and often more painful because of regular needle pricks and sometimes regular insulin injections. Appropriate treatment of diabetes decreases the long-term complications, but it does not usually make diabetics feel better; there is no immediate improvement in the quality of their lives. But when patients come to me and I diagnose depression, and when they are appropriately treated, the quality of life of most of them is significantly improved. Most feel back to normal or significantly better, and most are much more functional in day-to-day life academically, occupationally, and/or interpersonally. Most of the medications for depression do not have serious side effects; and although counseling is demanding, it, like medication, leads to an improved quality of life. In short, it is very gratifying to treat patients with depression since most soon feel so much better.

# 2

# Different Faces of Depression

WHEN TALKING ABOUT DEPRESSION, we face a problem with our nomenclature: The term *depressed* describes two very different problems. The word can be used for the common, mild, short-lived low moods most people experience from time to time. This same word is also used for people who are suffering from the mental illness called depression. "I am depressed" means something very different when used by people who have the mental illness called depression or, by contrast, those who do not have the mental illness called depression—those who are just discouraged. Most of the time I will be using the words *depressed* and *depression* in the sense of a mental illness.

Most people have three kinds of days: mountaintop days, plain days, and valley days. On mountaintop days, everything seems to be going great; the world looks bright. Most of life, for most people, consists of plain days, when we are not feeling exceptionally great, but neither do we have the blues or feel discouraged. Overall, we are doing pretty well. Valley days are gray days, when we have the blues or experience discouragement. On a valley day, we might say, "I am depressed" and not at all imply that we have a mental illness.

For people who have not experienced the mental illness called depression and are trying to understand it, it is helpful to recognize that depression is *not* just many gray valley days strung together. Depression, it is true, is one depressing day after another, on and on and on. The prolonged nature of the depression is part of the illness. There is indeed this *quan*titative component to depression. But in depression, there is also a *qualitative* component. For one, the mood is significantly worse than the blues or discouragement. The days are not merely gray. They are dark—sometimes pitch black. Secondly, there is a different character to the mood especially in more severe depression. Finally, there are many symptoms of depression unrelated to mood.

Severely depressed people often experience mental agony, prolonged despair with utter hopelessness, gripping fear, inner desperation, mental exhaustion, immobilizing apathy, debilitating helplessness, and regular thoughts of release from suffering by dying of natural causes or even by suicide. I have experienced all these symptoms many times, for prolonged periods of time. People with mild depression rarely experience these symptoms. However, moderate depression and especially moderately severe to severe depression is *qualitatively* different from discouragement and mild depression. Some say there is a continuum from mild to more severe depression but I believe something very different is experienced by those with mild depression and those with more severe depression.

## SYMPTOMATIC FACES OF DEPRESSION

There are many faces of depression. No two depressed people have exactly the same symptoms. Even the symptoms they share with others can have different qualities to them or are experienced to different degrees of severity. Here are some of the distressing symptoms depressed people may experience:

Clinically depressed people:

1. Often feel persistently sad and can be moved to tears by the most trivial circumstances. They may cry at the drop of a hat or for no reason at all. They are often excessively emotionally sensitive.

2. May feel empty. They may long to cry but be unable to. They may not even recognize that their feelings of emptiness are due to depression.

3. Often have loss of interest or pleasure in doing things. Things that used to bring happiness or satisfaction no longer do.

4. Often are anxious. They may be worried and tense most of the time, often precipitated by minor things, and be unable to put their anxiety aside.

5. May be restless, even agitated. Conversely, they may be sluggish and slow to react.

6. Often are poorly motivated and have to push themselves to do even the smallest task. Depression often feels like a vice squeezing out every drop of initiative.

7. May be demanding, difficult to please, and easily offended. This can, of course, lead to less social support, which depressed people really need.

8. May be irritable often with outbursts of anger, even rage. Small setbacks or frustrations may upset them. They may even think other people are trying to make life difficult for them. This irritability and/or anger can also lead to less social support.

9. May withdraw from social situations and show little emotion. In the elderly this apathy may be mistaken for dementia.

10. Often have trouble concentrating. They may be unable to watch TV, read a book, or engage on the internet.

11. Often have difficulty making decisions. Small decisions seem like overwhelming burdens. They may even avoid making important, necessary decisions.

12. May be very needy and dependent on others. They may be clingy, which can be emotionally draining and/or annoying to those trying to help. They may have a strong fear of abandonment.

13. May be pessimistic. The present and the future look bleak to them. Sometimes they remember the past to be worse than it really was.

14. May experience an erosion of appropriate self-esteem—appropriate self-worth.

15. Often have impairment of normal functioning at work, school, and home, especially in relationships.

16. May have frequent thoughts of dying, even committing suicide.

There are usually physical symptoms associated with depression, including the following:

1. Insomnia or its converse, hypersomnia (sleeping longer). Insomnia is the more common sleep disturbance with early morning awakening and frequent awakenings being the most typical. While awake in the night these insomniacs are often greatly tormented with fear and despair. Those who sleep longer than their normal sleep patterns do not feel refreshed when they wake up. Typically, the morning is the most difficult time of the day for depressed people.

2. Decreased appetite or its converse, increased appetite. Severely depressed people may lose or gain weight.

3. Physical fatigue and loss of energy. People often believe there is some nonpsychiatric cause of this fatigue and loss of energy.

4. Psychomotor retardation or its converse restlessness, even agitation. People may sit for long periods of time doing nothing and moving slowly when they do move. Conversely, they may literally pace the floors.

5. Sexual dysfunction, including decreased libido and erectile dysfunction or anorgasmia. These people may not even be bothered by their sexual dysfunction.

6. Symptoms associated with anxiety, such as breathlessness, palpitations, and dizziness. Most people with depression have anxiety.

7. Somatization. Somaticizing depressives have bodily symptoms that cannot be explained by a nonpsychiatric medical illness. Common psychosomatic symptoms include headache, abdominal pain, and numbness and tingling of the extremities. Psychosomatic symptoms are very real to the people who have them. They are not malingering. It is important for healthcare providers to recognize somaticizing depressives, to avoid unnecessary potentially dangerous testing and treatment.

If you find that you have one or two of the above twenty-three symptoms, you should not be concerned about having clinical depression. But if you have five or more, you may have depression and you should consider seeking help. In chapter 4 there is a screening form you can complete to see how likely you are to have clinical depression and if so, how severe.

## BODY AND SPIRIT: MATERIAL AND IMMATERIAL FACES OF DEPRESSION

Knowing about our nature as human beings (who we are), including our body and spirit, will better inform our understanding of depression and its treatment, from a biblical perspective. Early on we need to ask the question: "What are men and women made of?" In Genesis 2:7, we read, "Then the Lord God formed the man of dust from the ground and breathed into his nostrils the breath of life, and the man became a living creature."

Men and women have a material aspect to their being. Adam was created from "dust from the ground." Each person has a material, earthly body of which the brain is a part. Men and women also have an immaterial aspect to their being. "God breathed into [Adam's] nostrils the breath of life." Each person has a spirit that is the immaterial aspect of humankind's being. Thus, humankind is made of up of two elements: one is material (the body including the brain), and the other is immaterial (the spirit including the mind). Part of man (male and female) is dust, and part of man is God's breath. We will use the words *spirit*, *soul*, *mind*, and *heart* interchangeably in this book, which is linguistically justifiable, as there is significant overlap in their meaning in the Bible.

Genesis 2:7 also says that men and women are living creatures. The Hebrew word for *living creature* (also translated as "living being") is *nephesh*, which means an "embodied soul" or a "soul-filled body"; both are true—two sides of the same coin. There is a sort of duality of body and soul (the material and the immaterial), but in this earthly life the body is always fully united with the soul and vice versa. The brain is always united with a mind and vice versa. This union of the soul and body is what many call a psychosomatic unity. In the Greek, *psyche* (psycho) = soul/spirit, and *soma* (somatic) = body. In life on earth, the material and immaterial aspects of humankind are inextricably bound together. There is a *psyche-soma*, a psychosomatic, unity.

One analogy to the relationship between the material and immaterial aspect of humankind is the description of traditional landline telephone calls, which are now becoming obsolete. A particular telephone call can be described as sound waves, generated by human vocal cords, which are picked up by the telephone sound receptor. The sound is then converted into electrical activity that flows through the telephone wires to the sound receptor in another telephone. The sound receptor of the second telephone then converts the electrical activity back into sound waves received in the ear of the person answering the telephone call. This is one description of a landline telephone call. You can also describe the same telephone call as David called Mary and said to her, "I miss you! When can we get together again?" Both descriptions are true. Both are accurate descriptions of the telephone call. The telephone technology and the conversational speech are inextricably bound together. And so, it is that both the material and immaterial aspects of humankind are real and true and are inextricably bound together. We are embodied souls and soul-filled bodies.

Modern materialists reject the immaterial aspect of our being. The human soul, materialists believe, is nothing more than neurochemical dispersals and neuroelectric impulses. It is true that every thought, word, and action, including spiritual ones, have a physical component in the brain— including a chemical dispersal and an electrical impulse. But the human soul is more than material, more than the physical, more than the brain. The chemical and electrical activity are only part of the story. The other part is the immaterial aspect of the soul's activity. There are neurobiological (material) aspects of our lives, but there are also psychological and spiritual (immaterial) aspects. Depression involves the neurobiological, psychological, and spiritual aspects, and the treatment of depression should address all three.

Genesis teaches that each of us is a psychosomatic unity, but it also teaches that each of us is more than one body and soul, each alone in this world. We are, by nature, social beings as well as individuals. Genesis 1:27 reads, "So God created man in his own image, in the image of God he created him; male and female he created them." We are made in the image of God as men and women. Like the triune God (Father, Son, and Holy Spirit), we are made for relationships. In Genesis 2:18, God says, "It is not good that the man should be alone; I will make him a helper fit for him." Men and women are not made to be alone. When used elsewhere in the Bible, the Hebrew word for "helper" does not imply inferiority. In fact, "partner" may be a better translation. The word is most often used of God's relationship to us—he is most often our helper—our partner. Men and women need each other. Each needs to be the other's helper—the other's partner. There would be no meaningful telephone conversation if there weren't a relationship between two people. With this added biblical insight, we will in later chapters address the neurobiological, psychosocial, and spiritual aspects of depression.

## HISTORICAL FACES OF DEPRESSION

We can gain some insight into the different quality of the mood and other symptoms in clinical depression by looking at the life stories of severely depressed people from the past. Some of these men of faith struggled for years with debilitating depression. If this is your situation, please know that you are not alone in your journey.

### Two Western Writers

Two well-known Christian writers with recurrent severe depression give us glimpses into the mental pain of their oppressed, tormented minds: William Cowper and Charles Spurgeon.

*William Cowper*

William Cowper was a highly acclaimed eighteenth-century poet and hymn lyricist who suffered from recurrent, sometimes delusional, depressions, four of which resulted in complete mental breakdowns, some leading to institutionalization. During these terrible depressions, Cowper was frequently suicidal, sometimes imagining that God wanted him to commit suicide and then damn him to hell.

Cowper said of one of his depressions, "[I was struck] with such a dejection of spirits, as none but they who have felt the same, can have the least conception of. Day and night, I was upon the rack, lying down in horror, and rising up in despair." He also experienced depression as "terror . . . I am haunted by spiritual hounds in the night season."

Cowper was a sensitive six-year-old living in rural England when his mother died. He was immediately sent away to a boarding school he despised for two years; all the while he was homesick for his father. He was severely bullied by a much older boy, though we don't what kind of abuse he suffered.

Though he had little interest in his profession, early in Cowper's life he practiced law proficiently. When he was thirty-two and about to be promoted to a prominent government position, he became extremely fearful. This "horror," as he called it, was the beginning of his first severe, disabling depression. He came close to committing suicide in three ways: nearly taking an overdose of laudanum (an opiate), then considering stabbing himself with a knife, and then actually hanging himself with a garter strap that broke. Wisely, he was placed in an insane asylum (they were all that were available for the severely mentally ill in the eighteenth century).

For the next six months, Cowper felt like "a man when he arrives at the place of execution." The doctor at St. Albans Insane Asylum was a sincere Christian who enjoyed poetry. Dr. Cotton befriended Cowper and may have encouraged Cowper to read the Bible. One day the first verse Cowper read was Romans 3:25, part of one on the most powerful passages in Scripture, on justification of the sinner by faith in Jesus through his death on the cross. He was immediately, dramatically converted, and his depression lifted. Cowper said of that moment, "My eyes filled with tears, and my voice choked with transport."

After more than a year in the asylum, Cowper moved to the home of the Unwin family in Huntington, where he wrote poetry, though he was otherwise unemployed. Mary Unwin, eight years older than Cowper, became like a mother to him. John Newton (the one-time slave trader who wrote "Amazing Grace") was an Anglican priest serving in nearby Olney.

Newton cultivated a friendship with Cowper. Newton remained his friend for life despite what must have been a very emotionally demanding relationship. Cowper would later say of Newton, "A sincerer or more affectionate friend no man ever had."

Newton tried a number of ways to draw Cowper out of his melancholy (the word used for severe depression in the eighteenth century) and had some success when they wrote a hymnbook together. Most of Cowper's hymns were uplifting, beautiful, and profound. Cowper may have been thinking of himself when he wrote verse three of "There Is a Safe and Secret Place Beneath the Wings Divine":

> He [Cowper] feeds in pastures, large and fair,
> Of love and truth Divine;
> O child of God, O glory's heir,
> How rich a lot is thine.

But Cowper also wrote "My Soul Is Sad and Sore Dismayed." The most hopeful verse is the last, though it is still heavy with melancholy:

> Come, then, and chase the cruel host,
> Heal the deep wounds I have received.
> Nor let the powers of darkness boast,
> That I am foiled, and Thou art grieved.

Despite Mary Unwin's nurture and Newton's friendship, Cowper had another disabling, suicidal depression during this time of hymn writing.

After ten years as neighbors, Newton moved away but kept close touch with Cowper through many letters and some visits. The immediate six years after Newton's departure were some of Cowper's most productive years as a poet—writing both sacred and secular literature.

Cowper had two more disabling depressions—for a total of four—one almost every decade starting in his thirties. When Mary died, near the end of his life, Cowper entered a period of "fixed despair" from which he never recovered. His last poem, "The Castaway," is a heartbreaking memorial about a man falling overboard a ship in a storm. The first stanza is as follows:

> Obscurest night involv'd the sky
>    Th'Atlantic billows roared
> When such a destin'd wretch as I,
>    Washed headlong from on board.
> Of friends, of hope, of all bereft.
> His floating home forever left.

I have written on Cowper for two reasons: (1) I identify with so much of his life: heartbreaking boarding school; recurrent severe depressions that included terror, horror, and despair; friendships that have been lifesaving; and the gift of a deep abiding faith in God despite his mysterious, sometimes fearsome ways. The title of one of Cowper's most famous hymns is "God Moves in a Mysterious Way." (2) The second reason I identify with Cowper is that he is able to expresses his mental pain and joy in such beautiful, profound poems and hymns. He is able to speak to deep places in our souls whether we are depressed or not.

## Charles Spurgeon

Charles Spurgeon, who lived most of his life in nineteenth-century London, was one of the greatest Christian preachers of all time. He suffered from frequent severe depressions alternating with periods of incredible productivity. He may well have had bipolar 2 disorder, a form of bipolar disorder milder than bipolar 1 (more later). He certainly had a predisposition to depression. Spurgeon once said, and I am sure he included himself in his statement, "Some are touched with melancholy from their birth." Two of Spurgeon's physicians believed that part of the cause of his depressions was too much pressure from care and overwork. Waxing and waning chronic pain from "gout, rheumatism, and neuritis" also probably contributed to his depressions. Spurgeon was unable to preach one-third of his sermons due to depression and/or pain. Sometimes he was in such despair that the elders in his church had to practically push him into the pulpit. He was always dissatisfied with his sermon; he may have been a perfectionist. He seemed to be helped by sunny warm weather in the French Riviera, a respite from the cold, damp, and dark winters in London. Smoking daily cigars helped him. "I have found intense pain relieved, a weary brain soothed, and a calm, refreshing sleep obtained by a cigar." There may have been some humor in this assertion, as Spurgeon could be quite witty when he was not depressed. (I enjoy a good pipe smoke almost every day.)

Spurgeon's first of many depressions, at age twenty-two, was triggered by the death of seven people trampled in a panic when someone falsely yelled "fire!" during one of his sermons. His wife said, "My beloved's anguish was so deep and violent, that reason seemed to totter in her throne, and we sometimes feared he would never preach again." His critics predictably called his depression a judgment from God. Spurgeon's later depressions often did not appear to have such obvious triggers.

These are Spurgeon's own excerpts about depression:

"I could say with Job, 'My soul chooseth strangling rather than life.' I could have laid violent hands on myself to escape from my misery."

"My spirits were sunken so low that I could weep by the hour like a child, and yet I knew not what I wept for."

"There are dungeons beneath the Castle of Despair as dreary as the abodes of the lost, and some of us have been there."

"All mental work tends to weary and to depress, for much study is a weariness of the flesh."

"Depression of spirit is no index of declining grace; the very loss of joy and the absence of assurances may be accompanied by the greatest advancement in the spiritual life."

"Jesus is touched, not with a feeling of your strength, but of your infirmity."

I have written on Spurgeon for three reasons: (1) I identify with his alternation between periods of severe depression and periods of increased productivity (needless to say, mine are not nearly as productive as his); (2) overwork and prolonged study contributed to his depressions; (3) and, as with Spurgeon, depression has profoundly influenced my spiritual life.

## Two Biblical Heroes and a Psalm of Lament

At least two heroes of the Judeo-Christian faith seem to have been clinically depressed: the faithful, wise man Job and the prophet Jeremiah. Of course, we can't conduct a psychiatric interview with either of them, but we see present many of the symptoms of depression in both of them from biblical accounts. It also seems to me that their symptoms were severe and prolonged—more than a few days of discouragement.

Both are known to us as upstanding, holy men. God said of Job, "There is none like him on the earth, a blameless and upright man, who fears God and turns away from evil" (Job 2:3). The Lord told Jeremiah, the weeping prophet who wrote Lamentations, "Before you were born, I consecrated you [made you holy]" (Jeremiah 1:5). From the womb, God set Jeremiah apart for himself—"set apart" is a synonym for holiness.

It seems unlikely that the depressions of either of these two were due to sin or a lack of sufficient faith—a common misperception regarding depression among Christians. Of note is that neither of these heroes of the faith kept his story of depression to himself. Both made it public, in that we can read their accounts in the Bible today. Apparently, Job and Jeremiah were not ashamed to share their testimonies. Contrast their shared testimonies with those Christians today who hide their feelings of depression.

## Job

Job was not an Israelite, but he did know the Lord and much of what he said was consistent with Israelite wisdom literature at that time in history. The setting of Job's story is historically consistent with the time of the patriarchs, Abraham, Isaac, and Jacob. Satan believed Job feared God (feared God = reverently trusted and obeyed God) because God had so blessed him. Satan could not see into Job's heart—Satan can't see into our hearts either when God dwells in us. Job had ten children and many possessions that God allowed Satan to destroy as a test of Job's faithfulness to himself—what an awful test. Job's friends, who came to "comfort him," were later called by Job, "miserable comforters." In their theology, all troubles were punishment for wrongdoing; so, in their minds Job was being punished. In their application of this errant theology, Job needed to identify his sins and repent and then be blessed again. Job refused to accept this view of God's world and proclaimed his innocence. Despite his suffering, which included a severe depression, Job maintained his integrity and his faithfulness to God, saying, "Though he slay me, yet I will hope in him" (Job 13:15 KJV). (I think you remember that is the verse in my epitaph.)

In the end, Job's family and fortunes were restored and the Lord said to Job's friends, "You have not spoken of me what is right, as my servant Job has" (Job 42:7). The book as a whole illustrates three things: (1) There is no human answer to the question of how God can be just when the world is full of suffering; human beings see only a small part of any situation, and in the end the Creator God alone holds the answer of why there is suffering in the world. (2) Fully understanding God's reasons for allowing suffering is not a prerequisite for faithfulness to God; Job didn't even know he was being tested by the Lord through the agency of Satan. (3) Comfort comes not from having all the seemingly right theological answers. Rather, in my view, it is mostly about empathy and compassion, which so many depressed people desperately need.

It is not surprising that Job became severely depressed because of the distressing circumstances in his life—his many losses. In Job 3, the faithful, wise man Job expresses his depression by describing his feelings about the imagined day of his birth:

> Let the day perish on which I was born, and the night that said,
> "A man is conceived." Let that day be darkness! May God above

not seek it, nor light shine upon it. Let gloom and deep darkness claim it. Let clouds dwell upon it; let the blackness of the day terrify it. That night—let thick darkness seize it! Let it not rejoice among the days of the year; let it not come into the number of the months. Behold, let that night be barren; let no joyful cry enter it. (Job 3: 3–7)

A man who wishes he were never born is a troubled man indeed.

## *Jeremiah*

In Lamentations 1 and 3, Jeremiah, known as the weeping prophet, expresses his depression by noting and personalizing the Judeans' grief after the fall of Jerusalem and their exile to Babylon and Egypt. "For these things I weep; my eyes flow with tears; for a comforter is far from me . . . Look, O Lord, for I am in distress; my stomach churns; my heart is wrung within me" (1:16, 20). "My soul is bereft of peace; I have forgotten what happiness is; so, I say, 'My endurance has perished; so has my hope from the Lord'" (3:17–18).

## *Psalm of Lament*

Psalm 88 is a psalm of lament. It would have been regularly recited or sung in the worship life of the ancient Israelites.

O Lord, God of my salvation, I cry out day and night before you. Let my prayer come before you; incline your ear to my cry! For my soul is full of troubles . . . and you overwhelm me with all your waves. *Selah* . . . my eye grows dim through sorrow . . . O Lord, why do you cast my soul away? Why do you hide your face from me? Afflicted and close to death from my youth up, I suffer your terrors; I am helpless . . . You have caused my beloved and my friend to shun me; my companions have become darkness. (vv. 1–3, 7–9, 14–15, 18).

In this psalm, there is no sliver of joy, no ray of hope. The psalm even ends in despair: "my companions have become darkness." This psalm is a remarkable gracious gift to those who are severely depressed in despair and hopeless. It honors the relentless, painful thoughts and feelings of those who are severely depressed.

Among the Israelite worshipers, there would have been depressed individuals who could completely identify with Psalm 88. There would also have been empathetic worshipers who, though not depressed themselves, through this psalm would better understand the struggles of some fellow worshipers. The public recital of the psalm would surely have validated the feelings expressed and might have even lightened the burden of mental pain carried by those who were depressed.

We have seen that there are many faces of depression. We have also seen that some heroes of the Jewish and Christian faiths and more recent deeply committed Christians have suffered from depression. In none of their cases was the depression due to sin or a lack of faith. If you are depressed, you are in good company. You are, like me, a sinner saved by grace, but you are not depressed because you are a sinner.

# 3

## Genetic and Neurobiological Aspects of Depression

THE GENETIC AND NEUROBIOLOGICAL aspects of depression relate to the material aspect of our being—specifically the brain. In this very short chapter, we'll look at these two aspects. It is intrinsically dense material, but I have tried to make it understandable to the layperson.

### GENETIC PREDISPOSITIONS

Why depression manifests itself in some people and not in others is the subject of much research. It seems to have to do with a genetic predisposition to depression. We believe depressive genes often lie dormant until stressful situations stimulate the genes to express themselves in the form of symptoms of depression in some people. Significant psychological and environmental stress during childhood can be especially detrimental, often leading to a predisposition to depression later in life.

We are all endowed with a unique set of some 24,000 genes. Most of them are helpful, but some are hurtful—the earth and all that is in it is a broken creation. We have many genes in common with people outside our families. However, we have many more genes in common with our parents, whose combined set of genes make up our own. It is not surprising, then, that depression often runs in families. For genetic reasons, a person is three times more likely to experience depression if a close relative has experienced it. A person with bipolar illness, including bipolar depression, is five times more likely to have a close relative with the illness. Four out of five of my siblings and three out of four of my children have suffered from clinical depression. Neither of my parents had depression, but I have a great uncle, a brilliant inventor, who had "dark moods." In addition to the genetic influence, part of the increased rate of depression in some families is due to the psychosocial influence of parental depression and bipolar disorder on their children. Neither of my parents had depressive or bipolar tendencies, and I grew up in a happy home. I can't imagine what life would have been like for me if I had been raised in a troubled home.

For some people with genes predisposing them to depression, it takes only mild stress to trigger depressive gene expression. Others maintain an equilibrium until they encounter more severe stress. For me, relatively little stress can trigger a depression. An unfamiliar environment, prolonged intense study, and experiencing personal failure have triggered depression in me.

Some people do not have genes predisposing them to depression; even the most severe stress does not trigger depression in them. The late Senator John McCain, who spent several years in a North Vietnam POW camp, never suffered from depression. I'm sure that soon after arriving in South Vietnam I would have suffered from what was called "shell shock" or "battle fatigue" in previous wars. I'm so thankful that the Vietnam War draft ended the year I would have been drafted in the lottery. My birthday was number thirty-eight in the draft lottery that year, and I would have surely been sent to Vietnam if the United States had not pulled out of that unnecessary war.

Genetics may also play a role in the type of temperament we inherit. Differences in temperaments, such as fearfulness or oversensitivity to discipline, are often seen in infancy and early childhood. Some people just seem to be born with a sensitivity to rejection, loss, and multiple stressors, and fall prey to depression, even with exceptionally good parents.

Sometimes there are no apparent triggers for a depression. Neither ongoing chronic stress nor severe acute stressors are seemingly present. This type of depression is sometimes called endogenous depression. Much more often, however, chronic and/or acute stresses contribute to depression.

## NEUROBIOLOGY OF THE BRAIN

The neurobiology of depression and its treatment is extremely complex. If you don't care about how antidepressants and possibly counseling work at the neurobiological level—you just want to get better—skip this section.

We will address only a few of the most important neurobiological mechanisms thought to be important in causing and treating depression. Out of necessity I have simplified the mechanisms of actions to make them understandable to nonscientists. As an applied scientist, namely a physician, even I have difficulty understanding some of the known and hypothesized mechanisms of neurobiological action in depression and its treatment.

The chemical neurotransmitters released into the very tiny space called the synapse between two neurons (nerve cells) appear to be important in causing depression. A "chemical imbalance" of serotonin, norepinephrine, and dopamine in the synapse is a likely part of the mechanism of action of depression. Some psychiatrists think calling this part of the neurobiological cause of depression a "chemical imbalance" is an oversimplification, but I think it is a helpful, if simplified, lay description. The three neurotransmitters serotonin, norepinephrine, and dopamine, help regulate not only mood, but also sleep, appetite, sexual desire, and many other brain functions. There are certain areas of the brain that seem to me more influenced by serotonin; others more influenced by norepinephrine; still others more influenced by dopamine.

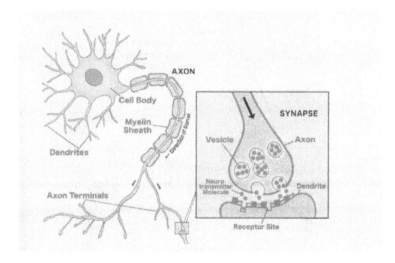

Above is a detailed microscopic picture of how nerve cells, called neurons, work in the brain. The dendrites (receiving tentacles) of the nerve-cell body (upper left corner) receive a chemical neurotransmitter message from another nerve cell. The chemical message is converted into an electrical message that is transmitted by an electrical impulse down through the axon of the nerve cell (middle left). The emitting axon terminals at the end of the axon (lower left) convert the electrical impulse back into the release of chemical neurotransmitters like serotonin, norepinephrine, and dopamine. These are stored in vesicles (magnified on the right in the box) in the emitting axon terminals. These chemicals are released from the vesicles into the narrow synaptic space between two nerve cells. The chemical neurotransmitter in the synapse then attaches to the receptor sites of the dendrites on the receiving nerve cell. Very soon after stimulating the receptor site, the chemicals are released back into the synapse. While the receiving nerve cell is sending its electrical impulse down the axon, the first nerve cell takes back up the chemicals from the synapse into its vesicles. This last process is called reuptake, and it regulates the amount of the chemicals in the synapse that can be attached to and reattached to the receptor sites of the receiving cell.

Most antidepressant medications are thought to work, at least in part, by the action of one or more of the neurotransmitters serotonin, norepinephrine, and dopamine. Most commonly, these antidepressants work by partially inhibiting the reuptake of one or more of these three neurotransmitters, which, as previously noted, help regulate not only mood, but also sleep, appetite, sexual desire, and other brain functions.

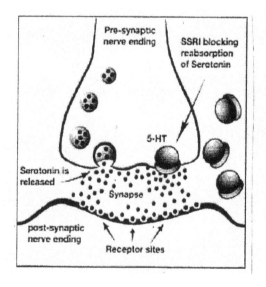

Serotonin (also called 5-HT) is one of the neurotransmitters released by the vesicles of the axon terminals into the synapse between two communicating neurons. This is how selective-serotonin reuptake inhibitors (SSRIs) work, the most commonly prescribed class of antidepressants, typical of about 80 to 90 percent of the all antidepressants I prescribe in practice. Selective serotonin-reuptake inhibitors (SSRIs) act by partially preventing the reuptake of serotonin into the vesicles of the transmitting nerve cell (see above). This results in more serotonin being present in the synapse and thus more being available to attach to the serotonin receptor sites of the dendrites of the receiving nerve cell. This helps, in laymen's terms, to restore the "chemical imbalance." Notice how it is an increase of our own serotonin that restores the chemical balance.

Some people worry that taking an antidepressant will change their personalities. This doesn't happen. It makes sense that an antidepressant wouldn't change one's personality since the antidepressant works by increasing the amount of a neurotransmitter that is already a part of a natural neurobiological mechanism of action. Rather than experiencing a personality change, most of those on antidepressants begin to feel like their old selves—sometimes even better than their old selves if they have experienced depression most of their lives.

Another likely important mechanism of action in depression and its treatment is the result of neuroplasticity. The brain has the ability to strengthen or weaken synaptic transmission. Microscopic structural changes can occur, including axon regeneration and new axon terminal sprouting, as well as dendrite growth and new dendrite formation. Restored or new axon terminals and dendrites may grow close together from opposite directions, thereby increasing the number of synapses in specific neural circuits of the brain. Whole new neurons and other brain cells can also increase in specific neural circuits. The opposite happens when synaptic transmission weakens. In depression, decreases in synaptic transmission may occur in certain neural circuits in the brain. It is believed that antidepressants and counseling work, in part, by strengthening synaptic transmission in neural circuits that are weakened by depression. It is also likely that some neural circuits in the brain of depressed people are overactive, like neural circuits responsible for mental pain and anger. Like synaptic reuptake inhibition, described above, this too is a simplification, but a useful one nonetheless. Neuroplastic changes in response to antidepressants and counseling may explain, in part, why improvement from depression comes on so slowly. Antidepressants and counseling take time to be effective.

PET scans make images of the brain's biochemical activity in different neural circuits. The brain on the left (see adjacent) is from a depressed person; the brain on the right is from a person with normal brain function.

## PET scan of the brain for depression

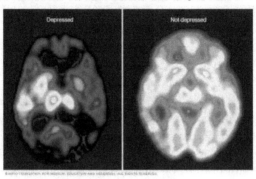

A PET scan can compare brain activity during periods of depression (left) with normal brain activity (right). An increase of blue and green colors, along with decreased white and yellow areas, shows decreased brain activity due to depression.

Different parts of the brain's neural circuits, especially in the limbic system and the prefrontal cortex, are associated with emotions, motivation, attention, memory, and decision-making, to name of few. Some parts of the limbic system and prefrontal cortex are more *inactive* in people who are depressed. These neural circuitry changes are due, in part, to changes in the microscopic structure of the brain. These changes often can be reversed if addressed early. Treatment with both antidepressants and counseling can stimulate desirable neuroplastic changes. However, the longer depression is ignored the harder it is to treat. Sadly, a few people with clinical depression who do not receive adequate treatment for very long periods of time may end up with some "brain damage" that is sometimes permanent. CT scans and MRIs (not shown here) show shrinkage of parts of the brain in some people who have suffered from prolonged severe depression. Please don't allow yourself to be one of them.

In the light of what was discussed above I often tell the depressed layperson that the biological cause of depression is due, in part, to chemical imbalances that affect some parts of the wiring of the brain. Antidepressants and counseling can help reverse these changes. This is a simplification but a helpful one. I have not found this simplification hurtful to depressed people, as some psychiatrists have suggested. It isn't everything that needs to be said about the cause of depression but it is helpful for depressed people to understand part of the neurobiological causes of depression and why medical treatment is helpful.

# 4

## Medical Diagnosis of Depression

OF THE VARIOUS TYPES of depression, we will here concentrate on the most common type, major depression. Much of what we discuss here also applies to the other types of depression. This is a long and demanding chapter, but if you can stick with it, you will be able to apply it practically to yourself and others you are concerned about.

### MAJOR DEPRESSION

**PHQ-2 Screening Instrument for Depression**

| Over the past two weeks, how often have you been bothered by any of the following problems? | Not at all | Several days | More than half the days | Nearly every day |
|---|---|---|---|---|
| Little interest or pleasure in doing things | 0 | 1 | 2 | 3 |
| Feeling down, depressed, or hopeless | 0 | 1 | 2 | 3 |

**Scoring:** A score of 3 or more is considered a positive result. The PHQ-9 (Table 3) or a clinical interview should be completed for patients who screen positive.

PHQ = Patient Health Questionnaire.

Adapted from Patient Health Questionnaire (PHQ) screeners. http://www.phqscreeners.com Accessed February 8, 2018.

Many primary care physicians, including me, use a brief screening tool to unmask major depression. It is called the PHQ-2 (Patient Health Questionnaire-2) screening instrument for depression. There are only two questions: over the past two weeks, how often have you been bothered by any of the following problems:

1. Little interest or pleasure in doing things

2. Feeling down, depressed, or hopeless

A score of 0 to 3 is assessed for each question based on the frequency of these symptoms. A total score of 3 or more is considered a positive screen for major depression.

Approximately 90 percent of people who have major depression will have a score of 3 or more. Only 10 percent of people with depression will be missed. But not all who have a score of 3 or more will be truly depressed. There are some false positives, that is, people who screen positive for major depression on the PHQ-2 but who don't really have depression. The ones who score 3 or more need to be further evaluated.

When I started using the PHQ-2 depression screening tool in my office, I was shocked at the number who had a score of 3 or more whom I would never have guessed were depressed. I would have missed more than half of them in a regular office visit if I hadn't done the screening. I've learned that many people with depression are good at masking it, and they don't tell their physician about their symptoms unless their physician asks.

A layperson can use an even simpler modification of the PHQ-2:

1. Do you have little interest or pleasure in doing things?

2. Have you been feeling down, depressed, or hopeless?

If someone says yes to either of these questions, that person should consider seeing a healthcare provider or a counselor. (See Appendix B for other brief, simple screening questions for mental illness.)

When I use the term *healthcare provider*, I am referring to psychiatrists, psychiatric nurse practitioners, primary care physicians, primary care physician assistants, and primary care nurse practitioners. When I use the term *counselor*, I am referring to psychologists and counselors who may have different counseling degrees and experience that qualify them to counsel those with mental illness—some of whom are clergy-trained in counseling for depression and other mental illnesses. Interestingly, most people with depression prefer going to a primary care healthcare provider than a psychiatric healthcare provider. They may feel more comfortable sharing their problems in a primary care setting, however, psychiatrists and psychiatric nurse practitioners are not healthcare providers to be frightened of.

I will usually use the terms *counselor* and *counseling* instead of *psychologist* and *psychotherapy*. They are close in meaning, but counselor and counseling sound less intimidating.

When a patient screens positive on the PHQ-2, the physician will often use a more detailed screening instrument called the PHQ-9 (Patient Health Questionnaire-9) primarily developed and researched by Robert Spitzer, MD.

### Patient Health Questionnaire-9 (PHQ-9)*

Patient Name: _____     Date: _____

Over the **last 2 weeks**, how often have you been bothered by any of the following problems? Circle your answers.

| | NOT AT ALL | SEVERAL DAYS | MORE THAN HALF THE DAYS | NEARLY EVERY DAY |
|---|---|---|---|---|
| 1. Little interest or pleasure in doing things | 0 | 1 | 2 | 3 |
| 2. Feeling down, depressed, or hopeless | 0 | 1 | 2 | 3 |
| 3. Trouble falling or staying asleep, or sleeping too much | 0 | 1 | 2 | 3 |
| 4. Feeling tired or having little energy | 0 | 1 | 2 | 3 |
| 5. Poor appetite or overeating | 0 | 1 | 2 | 3 |
| 6. Feeling bad about yourself or that you are a failure or have let yourself or your family down | 0 | 1 | 2 | 3 |
| 7. Trouble concentrating on things, such as reading the newspaper or watching television | 0 | 1 | 2 | 3 |
| 8. Moving or speaking so slowly that other people could have noticed. Or the opposite—being so fidgety or restless that you have been moving around a lot more than usual | 0 | 1 | 2 | 3 |
| 9. Thoughts that you would be better off dead or of hurting yourself in some way | 0 | 1 | 2 | 3 |

**FOR OFFICE CODING**       _____ + _____ + _____ + _____

= Total Score: _____

10. If you checked off **any** problems, how **difficult** have these problems made it for you to do your work, take care of things at home, or get along with other people?

| Not difficult at all | Somewhat difficult | Very difficult | Extremely difficult |
|---|---|---|---|
| ☐ | ☐ | ☐ | ☐ |

* Developed by Drs. Robert L. Spitzer, Janet B.W. Williams, Kurt Kroenke, and colleagues, with an educational grant from Pfizer Inc. Patient Health Questionnaire Screeners [Internet]. [Place unknown]: Pfizer; 2002–2016. GAD-7 Screener; n.d. [cited 2015]. Available from: http://www.phqscreeners.com

FOR CLINICIAN USE

*Patient Health Questionnaire-9 (PHQ-9)*

**SCORING LEGEND**

Major depressive disorder is suggested if:

1.  Question 1 or 2: Need 1 or both of the first 2 questions endorsed as 2 = "More than half the days" or 3 = "Nearly every day"
2.  Need a total of 5 or more of the 9 items endorsed within the shaded area of the form (questions 1–8 must be endorsed as a 2 or a 3; question 9 must be endorsed as a 1, a 2, or a 3)
3.  Question 10 must be endorsed as "Somewhat difficult," "Very difficult," or "Extremely difficult"

**USE OF THE PHQ-9 TO ASSESS SEVERITY AND MONITOR TREATMENT:**

Add the total score. The scoring interpretation is as follows:

0–4 = not depressed

5–9 = mild depression

10–14 = moderate depression

15–19 = moderate-severe depression

20–27 = severe depression

As we have said, if a patient screens positive on the PHQ-2 in the medical setting, we go to an expanded screening tool, the PHQ-9. The PHQ-9 can be self-administered or administered by the nurse or by the healthcare provider or counselor. The results of the PHQ-9, along with a medical/psychiatric interview, will confirm (or disconfirm) major depression and help assess its severity. Nine questions in the PHQ-9 refer to the overriding question, "Over the past two weeks, how often have you been bothered by any of the following problems?" (See the questionnaire, above.) Each of the nine questions is rated on a scale of 0–3 according to the frequency of the symptoms. The summed scores help determine if depression is likely and, if present, the severity of the depression. The symptoms must be at least "somewhat difficult" to live with. The scoring legend is detailed above. The scoring legend is a little complicated, but as a physician I use it to more accurately screen for and diagnose depression. Lay people can just add up the scores and get a sense of whether depression is likely and its severity. If depression seems to be present, an interview with a healthcare provider or counselor is in order to determine if depression is truly present. The PHQ-9 can lead to a small number of false negatives (people who screen negative on the form but really do have depression). If you screen negative on the self-administered PHQ-9 but still think you may be depressed, see a healthcare provider or counselor.

You may have heard about gene testing for depression. It does not help diagnose depression or tell you what antidepressant will work best, and it is fairly expensive. It does help the healthcare provider know whether a stronger or weaker dose of any antidepressant will be likely to be effective, but because most healthcare providers, including me, "start low and go slow," the testing may not be helpful.

## SUICIDE

Fourteen thousand Americans die every year from suicide, and at least 70 percent of them were depressed. Suicide is the second-leading cause of death in young people, especially males aged ten to twenty-four. Suicide is also more common in older men, especially those who are chronically and/or seriously ill and living alone. Asking about suicidal thoughts does not increase the risk of suicide. Most depressed people will appreciate your concern even if they are not suicidal.

Depressed people who die from suicide usually were suffering terribly and felt utterly hopeless. "Died from suicide" is a better expression than "committed suicide" since the later implies an action that comes from reasonable thinking. It is not a shameful thing when a depressed person dies from suicide; it is a tragedy. It is tragic that someone was in so much mental pain and felt so hopeless. It is also tragic that the suicide will almost invariably leave deep wounds in family and friends, and many of those wounds will never completely heal. The family and friends say to themselves: Why didn't I recognize how seriously ill my daughter was? Why didn't I do something that may have kept my son from suicide? Did I not let my wife know how much I needed her? Etc., etc.

There are many screening tools for suicide risk assessment. The Ask Suicide—Screening Questions (ASQ) works well in children, adolescents, and adults.

## ASK SUICIDE—SCREENING QUESTIONS

1. In the past few weeks, have you wished you were dead?

2. In the past few weeks, have you felt that you or your family would be better off if you were dead?

3. In the past few weeks, have you been having thoughts about killing yourself?

4. Have you ever tried to kill yourself?

5. Are you having thoughts of killing yourself right now?

A yes answer to question 3 or 4 and especially question 5 is, of course, much more serious than a yes answer to question 1 or 2. Thoughts of death are common during depression. Less common, but not rare, are thoughts of suicide, which are more dangerous. A yes answer to question 3 or 4 necessitates an assessment by a healthcare provider or a counselor on an urgent basis. A yes answer to question 5 necessitates assessment on an emergent basis, that is, immediately. This person may be actively suicidal and should be taken to the emergency room if he/she cannot be assessed emergently by a healthcare provider or counselor in his/her office. Often actively suicidal people need hospitalization until the risk of suicide diminishes. If nothing else, call the National Suicide Prevention Lifeline at 800-273-8255 or Google "suicide prevention." The Lifeline is open twenty-four hours daily seven days a week.

A final question should be asked if the answer to question 3, 4, or 5 is yes. Do you have a gun or enough pills to commit suicide? If the answer is yes, talk the person into temporarily giving a family member the gun to be placed in a secure place and a family member to safely store potentially lethal medications.

There are many risk factors for suicide. Here are five of the most important:

1. Previous suicide attempt

2. Current alcohol or other substance abuse (illegal and prescription drugs)

3. Marked anxiety

4. Social isolation

5. Hopelessness

It may be easier for laypeople to remember two questions to assess the risk of suicide (see Appendix B):

1. Have you recently had thoughts of killing yourself?

2. Are you considering killing yourself now?

An answer of yes to the first question lets you know if there are suicidal thoughts and an urgent assessment is in order. An answer of yes to the second question is an emergency requiring immediate evaluation. Do not let the potentially actively suicidal person out of your sight until he/she has been assessed for suicide risk by a healthcare provider or counselor. Sadly, suicide is often so impulsive that others do not have time to help. Nearly one quarter of suicide attempts occur within five minutes of considering it.

Self-harm, such as cutting or burning, may not be a suicidal act but a release from intense emotions or self-punishment. Often it is due to not knowing better ways to manage negative emotions. Still, it needs urgent attention.

## TYPES OF DEPRESSION OTHER THAN MAJOR DEPRESSION

### Persistent Depressive Disorder

Dysthymia (persistent depressive disorder) is a chronic depression lasting at least two years in adults and at least one year in adolescents. It is a daily or almost daily form of depression. It is not severe enough to prevent normal functioning in school or at work. Dysthymic people, however, have a pessimistic outlook and an inability to really enjoy life. They usually have low energy and to some degree feel guilty, helpless, hopeless, and/or worthless. They often withdraw socially and are passive in the few relationships they do have. Many have difficulty with assertiveness. Often these people can never remember a time in their lives when they did not have at least some of these symptoms. Sometimes dysthymic people will suffer from a major depression superimposed on their dysthymia. Called double depression, this is a particularly painful form of depression. Dysthymia can be treated with antidepressants and/or counseling; these are often helpful but usually do not result in a complete remission from symptoms. Antidepressants are particularly helpful in double depression.

### Seasonal Affective Disorder

Symptoms of depression sometimes begin or worsen as winter approaches—as the hours of darkness increase. This is called seasonal affective disorder (SAD). Symptoms often continue into the spring. Sometimes seasonal affective disorder occurs in night-shift workers or in cities where there is frequent cloud cover or air pollution. In addition to the usual treatment for major depression, light therapy may help. Sometimes antidepressants are only used during the problematic months.

## Premenstrual Dysphoric Disorder

Premenstrual dysphoric disorder (PMDD) is probably due to the effect on the brain of monthly hormonal changes. PMDD is characterized by depressed mood, irritability, and/or anxiety. The symptoms can be severe. They begin a few days to two weeks before menstruation and last until the start of menstruation. It may affect a woman's relationship with those close to her because of the dramatic mood changes that occur monthly, including irritability, which is sometimes severe. Fortunately, these symptoms can often be successfully treated with an antidepressant. In some of these patients, the antidepressant needs to be taken only before menstruation.

## Postpartum Depression

Postpartum blues are common. Thankfully postpartum depression is not nearly as common. Postpartum blues is less severe and usually lasts just a few days. Common symptoms include tearfulness, irritability, anxiety, and a sense of inadequacy. Postpartum depression is more severe and prolonged. On the one hand, most of the symptoms present in major depression are present in postpartum depression. On the other hand, some depressive symptoms overlap with normal postpartum changes such as fatigue, appetite change, low energy, and sleep problems. Because of this overlap, postpartum depression may be missed. In postpartum depression, there may be psychotic symptoms with obsessive thoughts about killing oneself and/or one's infant. The presence of obsessive thoughts and/or psychotic symptoms is a psychiatric emergency that often requires hospitalization until the symptoms subside. Treatments for major depression work well in postpartum depression. Electroconvulsive therapy (ECT) may be needed, especially in the presence of psychotic features or suicidal or homicidal thinking. Unfortunately, postpartum depression sometimes affects not only the mother but the infant as well due to problems in bonding.

## Depression in the Young

Depression in childhood and adolescence has some unique features. Only about 1 percent of preteen children in the United States experience depression. These children usually have more pronounced irritability than depressed mood, and they are often withdrawn. Visible anxiety, negative thinking, and angry outbursts are common. They may have academic difficulties and less involvement with peers. Many children with bipolar illness have rapid cycling from more depressive symptoms in the morning to more hypomanic or manic symptoms later in the day. It is confusing to the parent—it is as if their child has two different personalities. Treatment may include play therapy, which facilitates a connection between the behavioral health specialist and the depressed child. Not surprisingly, there almost always needs to be significant involvement of the parents, or some other caretaker, in the treatment plan.

About 13 percent of adolescents in the United States have a major mood disorder such as depression. There are often problematic relationships with parents including rebellious behavior, threats to run away from home, angry outbursts, and/or extreme sensitivity to criticism, to name a few. Disturbed relationships with peers may contribute to depression, for example, being bullied or humiliated. It is sometimes hard to differentiate depression from the normal moodiness of adolescents with their ups and downs of irritability and discouragement. In addition to the usual symptoms of depression found in adults, adolescents often have poor school performance, withdrawal from peers and peer activities, substance abuse, sexual promiscuity, problems with authorities, and aggressive risk-taking behavior. Hopelessness in adolescent depression is particularly worrisome because of the risk of suicide. A number of years ago, it was found that there were increased thoughts of suicide in depressed people younger than twenty-five years who took the antidepressant Prozac. There was no increase in actual suicides, but this concern led many physicians to quit prescribing antidepressants to younger patients. Sadly, this has led to inadequate treatment of many young people, and we are now seeing an increase in suicides among young people. The potential for increased suicidal thoughts needs to be addressed when prescribing antidepressants in young people, but we don't need to be concerned that antidepressants will increase the risk of completed suicides. In fact, they probably decrease the risk.

Parents, or other caretakers, need to be involved in the treatment loop with unemancipated minors. But most of the sensitive information shared between an adolescent and the healthcare provider or behavioral health specialist should remain confidential; otherwise, it is likely that the adolescent will not share relevant information. Always ask first to share information with parents. It is often difficult to know what should be shared with the parents when the adolescent doesn't want you to. A significant risk of suicide is an obvious reason to break confidentiality. Other issues are not as clear, for example, a problematic sexual relationship with a peer or a serious substance abuse problem. In the end, both the adolescent and his/her parents need to find a professional they trust.

## Depression in Seniors

Depression in the geriatric population has some unique features. Some loss of mental sharpness can be a symptom of normal aging or depression. Sometimes it is hard to differentiate depression from dementia. Both can result in memory problems, poor concentration, sluggish speech and movements, inattention to personal appearance, and apathy. It is also not uncommon for dementia and depression to occur simultaneously. Depression, dementia, and both simultaneously are very common in nursing homes (for as many as 50 percent of nursing home patients), and depression is especially problematic during the transition from relative independence to relative dependence in a new environment. If the symptoms are due to depression, they will resolve when the depression is treated. If there is uncertainty regarding the diagnosis, the person should be treated for depression, as treatment is so effective. Side effects from antidepressants are somewhat more problematic in older patients due to changes in body metabolism, so the dosages of medications initially used are usually lower than in younger patients.

## Depression Combined with Medical Illness

On the one hand, many medical illnesses increase the risk of depression. On the other hand, depression increases the risk of some medical illnesses. Medical illness combined with depression is common. Common medical conditions that increase the risk of depression include low thyroid hormone, low testosterone, heart attack, stroke, Parkinson's disease, cancer, HIV, diabetes, and chronic pain. Conversely, depression increases the risk of heart attack and stroke and increases the severity of chronic pain. When a medical illness is present, the depression should not be ignored; it should be treated as aggressively as it would be in an otherwise healthy person—in addition to treating the medical illness.

The negative effect of depression on some medical illnesses, such as diabetes and HIV, may be due in part to noncompliance to the treatment plan because of poor motivation, low energy, and/or hopelessness. Healthcare providers should try to motivate the patient to comply with treatment plans for the medical illness and the depression. Healthcare providers should also ensure that the side effects of the medications used for depression don't make the medical illness worse or vice versa. Drug interactions may complicate the treatment but almost always can be successfully managed. Sometimes the burden of taking care of a chronically ill person, such as someone with Alzheimer's or a severely disabled child, can contribute to depression in the caretaker.

## Depression and Substance Use Disorders

Depression often co-occurs with substance use disorders, especially alcohol, opioids including oxycodone and heroin, and stimulants including cocaine. Chronic opioid use and withdrawal often cause depression. Stimulant withdrawal often causes depression. Depressed people with opioid and/or stimulant addiction should usually be treated in inpatient or outpatient settings that specialize in "dual diagnoses."

Alcohol use disorder often occurs with depression and results in a significantly higher suicide rate than depression alone. Fourteen percent of people in the United States have had an alcohol use disorder in the past year. On the one hand, both heavy daily drinking and binge drinking can cause or contribute to depression. On the other hand, depression can lead to problematic alcohol use when the depressed patient uses alcohol to cope with depression. Some healthcare providers will treat depression only after the alcohol use disorder is effectively treated; this is called sequential treatment. Recently more healthcare providers treat alcohol abuse and depression at the same time; this is called integrated treatment. It seems that integrative treatment results in faster improvement in both alcohol use and depression. Special medications can be used to treat alcohol use disorder, alongside specific approaches to counseling. The medical treatment of the depression, however, is essentially the same, with or without problematic alcohol use. Unfortunately, alcohol dampens the body's response to antidepressants. Continued alcohol use can also increase the side effects of the antidepressant, and the antidepressant can increase the sedation of the alcohol. Use of tranquilizers like Valium, Ativan, Klonopin, and Xanax is fraught with problems in people with substance use disorders, including accidental or intentional overdose from the combination of alcohol and a tranquilizer.

## Bipolar Disorder

Up to 20 percent of people who suffer from major depression have bipolar disorder. In addition to depression, people with bipolar disorder have episodes of mania, mixed mania and depression, or hypomania. Depression without these additional symptoms is sometimes called unipolar depression. Bipolar patients often have their first depression or manic/hypomanic episode between fifteen and twenty-five years of age. There is often a family history of bipolar disorder. It is important to differentiate between bipolar and unipolar depression because they are treated differently. Here are the bipolar symptoms of mania, mixed mania and depression, and hypomania.

## Symptoms of Mania

A pronounced and persistent mood of euphoria (elevated or expansive mood) or irritability and at least three of the following:

1. Grandiosity or elevated self-esteem

2. Decreased need for sleep

3. Rapid, pressured speech (often these people are hard, if not impossible, to interrupt)

4. Racing thoughts

5. Distractibility

6. Increased activity or psychomotor agitation

7. Behavior that reflects expansiveness (lacking restraint in emotional expression) and poor judgment, such as sexual promiscuity, gambling, buying sprees, giving away money, etc.

## Symptoms of Mixed Mania and Depression

1. Marked irritability

2. Severe agitation or anxiety

3. Pessimism and unrelenting worry and despair

4. Significant suicide risk

5. Decreased need for sleep

## Symptoms of Hypomania

1. Increased energy and mental productivity

2. Decreased need for sleep

3. Talkative

4. Elated, mildly grandiose

5. Irritability

People who have had episodes of mania have bipolar 1 disorder. It is significantly more severe than people who have bipolar 2 disorder, with its episodes of hypomania. Bipolar 1 patients are usually unable to function at home or in school or at work. Bipolar 2 patients have milder symptoms and are usually able to function to some degree at home or in school or at work, though there are often interpersonal problems.

## Bipolar Screening

One can screen for bipolar disorder with two questions (see Appendix B):

1. Have you ever had periods of increased energy?

2. Have you ever had periods of decreased need for sleep?

In question 2, a "yes" refers to having significantly less sleep and not needing it. If the answer is yes to either question, the person should be assessed in more detail by a healthcare professional or counselor, often with the help of the Mood Disorder Questionnaire (MDQ) primarily developed and researched by Robert Hirschfeld, MD.

Here are the thirteen questions from the MDQ:

Has there ever been a period of time when you were not your usual self and . . .

1. you felt so good or so hyper that other people thought you were not your normal self, or you were so hyper that you got into trouble?

2. you were so irritable that you shouted at people or started fights or arguments?

3. you felt much more self-confident than usual?

4. you got much less sleep than usual and found you didn't really miss it?

5. you were much more talkative or spoke much faster than usual?

6. thoughts raced through your head or you couldn't slow your mind down?

7. you were so easily distracted by things around you that you had trouble concentrating or staying on track?

8. you had much more energy than usual?

9. you were much more active or did many more things than usual?

10. you were much more social or outgoing than usual; for example, you telephone friends in the middle of the night?

11. you were much more interested in sex than usual?

12. you did things that were unusual for you or that other people might have thought were excessive, foolish, or risky?

13. spending money got you or your family in trouble?

If you have only one or two of these symptoms, you do not need to worry about having a bipolar disorder. People with bipolar disorder will have several of these symptoms and will have them simultaneously, that is, all at the same time. Those with seven or more of these symptoms simultaneously, causing a moderate to severe problem at home, at work, and/or socially, are likely to have bipolar 1 disorder. Those with bipolar 2 may have fewer symptoms simultaneously and/or the symptoms will cause less severe problems in work, school, home, and/or relationships. The diagnosis of bipolar disorder is not made on the basis of the MDQ alone. The diagnosis requires evaluation by a healthcare provider or counselor.

## Depression and Its Relationship to Anxiety

Whenever depression is diagnosed, anxiety should be looked for as well. In the medical literature it is often stated that anxiety co-occurs with depression 60 percent of the time. In my practice the co-occurrence seems much more common. Anxiety is an inner feeling of apprehension, uneasiness, worry, and/or fear that is often associated with physical symptoms such as dizziness, heart palpitations, shortness of breath, and muscle tension. Anxiety can be a normal response to a situational threat when the response is proportional to the level of danger. Anxiety in someone who is threatened by violence or other life-threatening situations is a healthy response. Anxiety becomes an illness when the feelings are exaggerated and/or the threats are minimal or nonexistent. The illness of anxiety can make concentration difficult, cause impaired memory, affect school or job performance, and strain relationships just like depression can. When the anxiety is related to a specific circumstance, is relatively mild, and is short-lived it is sometimes called adjustment disorder with anxiety.

Anxiety can be caused by depression, or depression can be the effect of anxiety, or both. If the symptoms of anxiety begin with the onset of depression, it is likely that depression is the cause of the anxiety. In this case, the major focus should be treating the depression, which usually results in marked improvement in the anxiety. If anxiety predates the depression, there is often an underlying anxiety disorder. The stress from anxiety disorders can contribute to depression, so the anxiety disorder should be treated in addition to the depression.

All the symptoms of anxiety that are caused by depression are also seen in generalized anxiety disorder (GAD). The generalized anxiety disorder 7 (GAD-7) was primarily developed and researched by Robert Spitzer, MD as a screening tool for generalized anxiety disorder (GAD). The symptoms can occur with or without symptoms of depression.

## General Anxiety Disorder 7

**GAD-7***

Patient Name: _____    Date: _____

| OVER THE LAST 2 WEEKS, HOW OFTEN HAVE YOU BEEN BOTHERED BY THE FOLLOWING PROBLEMS? (USE A "✔" TO INDICATE YOUR ANSWER) | NOT AT ALL | SEVERAL DAYS | MORE THAN HALF THE DAYS | NEARLY EVERY DAY |
|---|---|---|---|---|
| 1. Feeling nervous, anxious, or on edge | 0 | 1 | 2 | 3 |
| 2. Not being able to stop or control worrying | 0 | 1 | 2 | 3 |
| 3. Worrying too much about different things | 0 | 1 | 2 | 3 |
| 4. Trouble relaxing | 0 | 1 | 2 | 3 |
| 5. Being so restless that it is hard to sit still | 0 | 1 | 2 | 3 |
| 6. Becoming easily annoyed or irritable | 0 | 1 | 2 | 3 |
| 7. Feeling afraid as if something awful might happen | 0 | 1 | 2 | 3 |
| **Add the score for each column** | 0 | + | + | + |
| **Total Score** | | | | |

If you checked off any problems, how difficult have these made it for you to do your work, take care of things at home, or get along with other people?

Not difficult at all _____

Somewhat difficult _____

Very difficult _____

Extremely difficult _____

Scoring

0–4 no anxiety/remission

5–9 mild anxiety

10–14 moderate anxiety

>15 severe anxiety

In addition to screening for generalized anxiety disorder, the GAD-7 is also useful for determining how severe the anxiety is in a depressed patient.

The GAD-7 form is similar to the PHQ-9 form. The seven questions in the GAD-7 refer to the overriding question, "Over the past two weeks, how often have you been bothered by any of the following problems?" The seven questions are listed above. Each question is rated on a scale of 0–3 according to the frequency of the symptoms. The scores are added up and help determine if anxiety is present and, if present, its severity. The symptoms must be at least somewhat difficult to live with.

Laypeople may want to use the following even briefer screen for anxiety (see Appendix B):

1. Do you feel nervous, anxious, or on edge?

2. Are you not able to stop or control your worry?

## Four Other Anxiety Disorders

There are four anxiety disorders other than generalized anxiety disorder (GAD): panic disorder, social anxiety disorder, obsessive-compulsive disorder, and post-traumatic stress disorder (PTSD). All these disorders are more common in people with depression. Fortunately, all four can often be effectively treated, at least partially, with counseling and/or medication. I believe counseling should always be a part of the treatment regimen in anxiety disorders. Here are brief descriptions of the four:

1. *Panic disorder* involves frequent panic attacks that have a sudden on-set and last ten to thirty minutes. The symptoms include intense fear and dread, with physical symptoms of anxiety such as heart palpitations, shortness of breath, and dizziness. In between these panic attacks, there is significant anticipatory anxiety—fear of another panic attack. This anticipatory anxiety often keeps the sufferer from doing some things for fear of precipitating another panic attack. The person often avoids situations where they previously experienced a panic attack. With each panic attack in a new situation slowly their world gets smaller and smaller. Agoraphobia is a more severe form of panic disorder that often keeps people housebound.

2. *Social anxiety disorder* makes people feel very anxious about engaging in social activities, especially in unfamiliar situations. They are often anxious that they will be negatively perceived by others. They especially fear speaking in public, being concerned that they will be

humiliated by something they do or say. This problem can keep people from advancing in their career.

3. *Obsessive-compulsive disorder (OCD)* exhibits itself by intrusive (obsessive) thoughts and repetitive behaviors (compulsions) like hand washing or repeatedly checking on things; some even recite numbers in their heads. These people get very anxious if they can't control their intrusive thoughts or perform their repetitive behaviors. However, performing the repetitive behaviors only results in brief relief of anxiety, after which the cycle of intrusive thoughts and repetitive behaviors starts all over again. OCD can be very debilitating.

4. *Post-traumatic stress disorder (PTSD)* can occur with people who have personally experienced or have witnessed a very traumatic event, such as being the victim of rape or seeing a death of a war comrade. These people have frequent, distressing recollections of the event—frightening memories, flashbacks, and nightmares that cause extreme anxiety. They avoid situations that remind them of the trauma.

We have seen ways that help screen for and diagnose major depression, suicide risk, bipolar disorder, and anxiety disorders (see Appendix B for brief screening questions). If you screen positive for any of the above, it is time to get help. There is so much that can be done for these problems. Make an appointment with a healthcare provider or a counselor.

# 5

## Medical Treatment of Depression

I AM INDEBTED TO the authors of *Clinical Psychopharmacology: Edition 8* for some of the information in this chapter and Appendix A. I have, however, put the information in my own words. I also include important information from many other sources including some in my Selective Bibliography.

There are two main approaches to treating major depression: (1) medical treatment, especially antidepressant medications, and (2) counseling. Treatment of major depression with either one (antidepressants) or the other (counseling) or both together has been shown repeatedly in many rigorous research studies to:

1. shorten current depressive episodes

2. decrease psychosocial impairment

3. decrease risk of suicide

4. increase quality of life

5. decrease relapse rate

Many experts believe that mild depression should be treated with psychotherapy alone; if the symptoms worsen, antidepressants can be prescribed. Another approach in mild depression is watchful waiting by monitoring symptoms to see if they resolve spontaneously without any treatment. If watchful waiting is chosen as the management strategy, the depressed person should be educated about symptoms that would necessitate a reevaluation. For moderate depression, antidepressant medications alone or counseling alone are often effective. Many experts, however, recommend using both. I certainly do. Most of these experts also believe that using antidepressants should almost always be part of the treatment plan for moderately severe and severe depression.

In the rest of this chapter, we'll address medical treatments for depression and bipolar disorder including bipolar depression. Detailed information on specific antidepressants is found in Appendix A. If you are on an antidepressant or your healthcare professional is going to prescribe one, you can look it up in this appendix. In chapter 9, we will look at two common counseling approaches that have been shown to be effective in many research studies.

If you are suffering from depression and are not currently being treated with an antidepressant, I hope you will see how safe and effective many of the medical treatments are—how many treatment options are open to you. I also hope it will take some of the mystery out of the medical treatment of depression. If some antidepressants have not been effective for you in the past, you will see what other options are available. If you have been previously treated with an antidepressant and had unacceptable side effects, you will also be able to see what other medication options don't have those side effects or not to the same degree.

Antidepressants are very effective. For example, 50 to 70 percent of depressed patients placed on their first SSRI (more later) will note significant improvement in four to eight weeks.

There are three things that antidepressants are not. (1) They are not happy pills that everyone should take. If you do not have depression, you will not get happier taking them. However, if you have depression and you are down or depressed you will likely get happier. (2) They are not addicting. If you stop some antidepressants abruptly, you may have relatively mild, short-lived discontinuation symptoms such as nausea, anxiety, insomnia, malaise, and electrical shock-like feelings in your body. Most antidepressants should be weaned off incrementally so there are no discontinuation symptoms. (3) Most antidepressants are not expensive. Many are very inexpensive (as little as $4.00 per month) and generic forms of antidepressants are often just as effective as brand names.

Given our understanding of the neurobiology of depression, it is not surprising that medical treatment of the biological component of depression helps. It grieves me that many people reject the use of antidepressants that so often help and are especially needed in moderately severe to severe depression. Many who choose not to use an antidepressant suffer needlessly and may develop the changes in the brain function and anatomy discussed earlier. Antidepressants are no panacea; a significant minority of patients are not helped or are only helped in part. But people who have not been helped by antidepressants do no favor by leading other depressed people to believe that no depressed people, or only a few, are helped by these medications. There is no excuse for counselors to downplay the helpfulness of antidepressants. I have heard counselors claim that antidepressants don't cure depression—they only help the symptoms. This is a ridiculous comment, as depression is defined by a constellation of symptoms, not by some other means like a physical exam finding or a blood test. If an antidepressant has resulted in the remission of all the symptoms of depression, which often occurs with medical treatment alone, the illness of depression has ended. I'm not saying that counseling is not important. It is, but medications really do help most of the time. Also, some counselors exaggerate the side effects of antidepressants (more later).

It is well known that part of an antidepressant's effect is its placebo effect. Just taking a pill, especially if you have confidence in a prescriber who shows real concern for you, often improves depressive symptoms. Because of the placebo effect, some argue against the use of antidepressants, but they do have significant efficacy beyond that of the placebo effect. When one of my depressed patients improves on an antidepressant, it doesn't matter to me whether it is the placebo effect or the effect of the medication or both. It is impossible to tell. What matters to me is that their mental pain and suffering are being relieved.

There are four antidepressant classes of reuptake inhibitors: (1) There are seven selective serotonin reuptake inhibitors (SSRIs) that inhibit the reuptake of only serotonin. (2) There are five inhibitors (SNRIs) that inhibit the reuptake of serotonin and norepinephrine. (3) There is only one norepinephrine and dopamine reuptake inhibitor. (4) There are many tricyclic antidepressants but only five are prescribed with any degree of frequency today. Tricyclic antidepressants work in part on the reuptake of serotonin and/or norepinephrine. Tricyclic antidepressants are not used frequently today because they have more side effects than most other antidepressants.

The effectiveness of most antidepressant medications is comparable across classes. With your input, your healthcare provider will determine which antidepressant medication is right for you. Your provider will take into account the antidepressant side-effect profile, drug interactions, cost, co-occurring psychiatric and medical conditions, and previous response to a specific antidepressant taken by yourself or the response of a close family member. One plant substance, St. John's wort, has SSRI antidepressant properties, but I do not recommend it because it is not approved by and regulated by the Federal Drug Administration. More on St. John's wort can be found in Appendix A.

There are numerous compounds on the market with no proven efficacy for depression. Many depressed people, desperate for relief, will try anything to get better. Some people who take these compounds do improve, but not necessarily because of the medicine's effect. Some improve because of the spontaneous healing course of most depressive episodes over time. Other people on these compounds improve because of the treatment's placebo effects. Thinking something will help, as we have said, often does help, so I am not opposed to using them if they are safe. Unfortunately, the safety of many alternative medicine remedies has not been sufficiently studied, and they are not well regulated in terms of efficacy and potency.

I think it is erroneous to believe that something "natural" is better than something manufactured. We live in a fallen world where many "natural" things are useless at best or harmful at worst. In my opinion, science is better at sorting out the benefits and risks of a treatment than the sloppy way the benefits and risks are assessed for many alternative medicine products. Unfortunately, there is not much valid, rigorous research being performed on alternative medicine remedies. Most of the funding for good research of treatments for depression comes from pharmaceutical companies trying to sell their product—often expensive, new medications. There is, sadly, much less money available for research of alternative medicine remedies. Most people who take a "natural" antidepressant do so on the basis of fake research and/or the testimony of its effectiveness by someone they know or have read about. They base their decision to take a remedy on anecdotal evidence, which is notoriously inaccurate. However, if you are on one that is safe and you are getting better, I would not advise going off of it regardless of why it is effective.

Many depressed people are afraid of the side effects of antidepressants. I can assure you that for the antidepressants most commonly prescribed today the side effects are almost always mild and easily reversible. The side effects are rarely severe and extremely rarely life-threatening. Most patients have no side effects at all. (Refer to Appendix A for the side effects of various antidepressants.) Some antidepressants may have mild side effects such as nausea and diarrhea at first that resolve in one to two weeks. There is often a mild increase in anxiety at first that steadily decreases after one to two weeks. Eventually there is a decrease in anxiety from baseline as the antidepressant takes effect. If you experience agitation you should let your healthcare provider know since it may be the result of the antidepressant. Some, not all, can contribute to weight gain. Some, not all, can lead to reversible sexual dysfunction. Some are energizing and some are tranquilizing. Some help insomnia, and some can make it worse (again usually short term). Some can cause reversible apathy. I want to reinforce that most patients experience no or only mild, short-lived side effects. If you have an intolerable side effect, your healthcare provider can decrease your dose or switch to an antidepressant with a different side-effect profile.

When prescribed, an antidepressant will take at least two weeks for improvement to begin and four to eight weeks for maximum improvement at any given dose. This delay in effect is terribly distressing to patients and is a frequent reason for stopping an antidepressant. The patient needs to understand that there will be a delay. I increase the antidepressant dose if the patient has not had even slight improvement in two weeks or significant improvement after four weeks at any given dose.

When an antidepressant brings about only a partial remission, your healthcare provider may choose to continue it and add on another medication, which may be another antidepressant or a non-antidepressant augmenting medication. Common antidepressant combinations include SSRIs or SNRIs in combination with bupropion, mirtazapine, or trazodone (see Appendix A). Common augmentation strategies include adding a mood stabilizer such as lithium or an atypical antipsychotic, or an activating medication like Cytomel or Ritalin (see Appendix A).

Fifty percent of people who have one major depression will have a recurrence; 70 percent of people who have two major depressions will have a recurrence; 90 percent of people who have three major depressions will have a recurrence. Most experts believe that antidepressants should be continued for life after the second or third major depression, especially if the depressions were moderately severe or severe. The first depression should be treated for six to nine months after symptoms fully remit. If the first depression is particularly severe or prolonged, lifetime treatment with an antidepressant should be considered. There are no known significant long-term side effects from antidepressants. Counseling during and after a major depression also reduces the risk of recurrence.

Here are some suggestions toward getting the most out of antidepressant treatment:

1.  Do not get discouraged if you do not note improvement in the first two weeks. It may take four weeks or more to get substantial improvement at any given dose. If there is no substantial improvement at four weeks the dose is usually raised over time to a maximum dose before switching to another antidepressant.

2.  The first symptoms to improve include improved sleep, increased energy, and better emotional control. Other symptoms may take longer to resolve, including the troubling symptoms of depressed mood and/ or loss of interest or pleasure.

3. Do not give up on antidepressants altogether because of intolerable side effects from one. Your healthcare professional can help you with dosage adjustment or switch you to another medication with a different side-effect profile. Remember, most people experience no side effects at all.

4. Do not stop your medication when you get better. You should be on the medication at least six to nine months after you are better, or you may soon relapse. If your depression is your second one or more, or if you had a particularly severe depression, you may need medications for life to prevent recurrence. Of course, you don't have to take it for life if you are willing to take the substantial risk of recurrence.

5. Antidepressants are not addictive, but you may have to come off of them slowly to prevent discontinuation symptoms. This is especially true with paroxetine (Paxil) and venlafaxine (Effexor).

6. Do not drink alcohol (or limit it to one drink per day), as it antagonizes the effects of antidepressant medications. If you can't limit yourself to one drink per day don't drink at all.

7. Limit caffeinated beverages to two cups per day and only in the morning.

8. If your medication is too expensive, ask a different pharmacy if it can fill your prescription at a lower cost or ask your healthcare provider for a cheaper type of antidepressant. Another trick to paying less is to get a stronger dose and cutting the pill in half (this doesn't work for capsules).

## TREATMENTS FOR BIPOLAR DEPRESSION

Bipolar depression (*with* episodes of mania, mixed mania and depression, or hypomania) is treated differently from unipolar depression (*without* episodes of mania, mixed mania and depression, or hypomania). Treating with an antidepressant alone can trigger manic, hypomanic, and mixed manic and depressive episodes in bipolar people. The mainstay of treating bipolar depression is mood stabilizers. They help with bipolar depression and prevent, at least partially, the episodes of mania, mixed mania and depression, and hypomania. Bipolar patients are often noncompliant, in part because they enjoy being hypomanic. They don't seem to remember how dysfunctional they were when they were manic. They also don't seem to remember how depressed they were before they improved. I do not believe counseling alone is adequate treatment for bipolar disorder.

There are three classes of mood stabilizers. Lithium is in a class by itself. Atypical antipsychotics are a second class of mood stabilizers, like the relatively inexpensive olanzapine (Zyprexa), quetiapine (Seroquel), and aripiprazole (Abilify), and the expensive lurasidone (Latuda and Invega). There are many other atypical antipsychotics in between the least expensive and the most expensive. Antiseizure medications, such as lamotrigine (Lamictal), divalproex (Depakote), and carbamazepine (Tegretol) are a third class that are all inexpensive. Though it is controversial, I believe that sometimes an antidepressant may be cautiously added if bipolar depression persists after the mood has stabilized in a patient with bipolar 2 and occasionally bipolar 1. For specific treatments and side effects see Appendix A.

## MEDICAL TREATMENTS OTHER THAN MEDICINES

There are a number of medical treatments for depression that do not involve taking medicine, including transcranial magnetic stimulation, electroconvulsive therapy, vagal nerve stimulation, and deep brain stimulation.

Transcranial magnetic stimulation (TMS) involves repetitive pulsation from electromagnetic coils placed on the scalp, which may work by activating nerve cells in the region of the brain that has decreased activity due to depression. It is often used after failure of antidepressant treatments or in patients resistant to taking psychopharmacologic medications. It requires three sessions per week for four to six weeks. Its only significant side effects are a mild headache or light-headedness. There are no severe side effects. Because of equipment and technician cost, it is somewhat expensive. Recently, however, more insurance companies will pay all or part of the cost.

Electroconvulsive therapy (ECT) is not commonly used, but it is especially helpful in depressed people who: (1) are severely depressed and have psychotic features (out of touch with reality often with hallucinations and/or delusions), (2) are actively suicidal (the risk of suicide dramatically drops after ECT), or (3) are severely depressed and have been unsuccessfully treated with several adequate antidepressant treatment regimens. ECT is not a painful or unpleasant procedure. The movie *One Flew Over the Cuckoo's Nest* showed ECT as it was used in the past and extremely exaggerated the side effects of ECT. As ECT is currently used, the patient is given a short-lived anesthetic to make him/her unconscious and a muscle relaxant to prevent physical manifestation of the muscle spasms of a seizure. The electrical shock from electrodes placed on the scalp produces a brief seizure of the brain. The only common side effects of ECT are a mild headache and memory loss. Usually, the memory loss is of events just before and just after the treatment that may last for a few days. Uncommonly, there is permanent loss of memory of events around the time of the ECT. Treatments are usually given three times per week for six to twelve sessions. ECT is highly effective. Whereas the first SSRI used is at least partially effective 50 to 70 percent of the time after four to eight weeks, ECT is 80 to 90 percent effective after one to three weeks, if it is the first treatment used for depression. This positive effect is in spite of the fact that the patients are usually more severely depressed. A research study has shown that most patients who have had ECT would do it again if their psychiatrist recommended it for a subsequent depression. I have had three series of ECT, and I would be happy to have it any time I am experiencing severe depression. It is expensive because it is labor intensive, requiring psychiatrist, anesthesiologist, and nurse time, and room time in specialized places in the hospital. Again, medical insurance often pays for part or all of the cost.

Vagal nerve stimulation and deep brain stimulation are invasive and infrequently used. They can be used when all else fails and are often effective. They can have uncommon serious side effects, but they may be worth the risk for those with severe treatment-resistant depression.

There are many effective medical treatments for depression, many inexpensive and with few side effects. If some are too expensive or have intolerable side effects for you, there are many other options. Many treatments do not work immediately so you have to be patient, which is really hard to do when you are suffering from depression.

## HOSPITALIZATION

Sometimes depression is so severe or the depressed person is at such high risk for suicide or homicide, that hospitalization is necessary. Hospitalization is often frightening to the depressed person. I have been hospitalized twice for depression and I am thankful I was both times. To follow is a description of hospitalization for depression on a modern psychiatric unit. I share it with you so that you can know what to expect if you need to be hospitalized. It comes from the book *Downcast,* written by three psychiatrists from a Christian perspective.

*On the inpatient psychiatric unit, all patients are closely monitored in order to minimize risk to and from themselves and others. This may involve checks every fifteen minutes by staff members or a staff member sitting with a patient at all times for patients at higher safety risk.*

*Upon arrival to the unit, most patients are observed for a period of time to ensure safety before they earn privileges to leave the unit on supervised walks or breaks. Visitors are typically allowed according to each unit's visiting hours and rules. To ensure the safety of all patients, personal belongings may be searched. Once items have been searched, patients are typically allowed to wear their own clothing.*

*While on the unit, patients receive a full medical and psychiatric evaluation, including a diagnostic interview with a psychiatrist, blood tests and other assessments as necessary. This evaluation, along with continued assessment by staff throughout the hospitalization, ensures an accurate diagnosis is made. Clinicians then recommend interventions accordingly, including medication and/or behavioral or cognitive strategies* [more later on this in chapter 9]. *Patients are also encouraged to participate in various therapy groups and recreational programs available on the unit daily. Participation in these activities can help optimize the therapeutic value of hospitalization.*

*In addition to speaking with psychiatrists, patients also have frequent contact with mental health counselors, nurses and social workers. Each of these professionals helps to monitor patient progress, and the entire treatment team meets often to discuss and adjust each patient's treatment plan. Most units have a chaplain available, and patients may request to have their own priest, pastor or church elder visit.*

*A major advantage of hospitalization over outpatient care is that both medication adjustment and psychotherapy can be conducted in a more intensive manner, due to the more frequent contact with mental health professionals and the close oversight of staff at all hours. Medication changes can be made more rapidly, and serious side effects [these are rare] can be immediately detected. Other advantages include that the patient is kept safe (from harm inflicted on self and others) due to staff monitoring, and the patient can have a reprieve from outside factors that may have been contributing to depression or distracting from depression treatment. For patients who may need electroconvulsive therapy (ECT), the hospital is often an ideal place to prepare for and undergo treatments.*

# 6

## Commonsense and Alternative Medicine Treatment of Depression

THERE ARE A NUMBER of commonsense approaches to the treatment of depression that should not be the primary means of treating depression but might add to the effectiveness of treatment. I will address sleep, diet, and exercise. Some research indicates that these lifestyle modifications can prevent or improve depression. These lifestyle changes are not my primary approach to treating depression, but they may be good as adjuncts to treatment. I'll then briefly discuss mindfulness with or without an accompanying physical component, which is getting more attention in recent days.

### MODIFYING THREE LIFESTYLE HABITS

#### Sleep

Insomnia is a common symptom of depression. Insomnia can make daytime coping with depression and anxiety much more difficult. Even nondepressed people can get irritable, have difficulty focusing, and become more pessimistic if they don't get adequate sleep. Good sleep habits can sometimes ameliorate the insomnia associated with depression. Here are some recommendations for good sleep hygiene:

1. Go to bed at the same time and get up at the same time every day. Seven to nine hours of sleep is ideal.

2. Do not read, watch TV, or use your computer or smartphone when you're in bed. Bed should be reserved for sleep and intimacy.

3. Limit caffeine to two cups per day and only in the morning. Among other things, caffeine affects the quality of sleep, as does alcohol after supper. One alcoholic drink with supper is probably all right but no more. Although alcohol can have the immediate effect of bringing on sleep, it affects the quality of sleep. Again, if you cannot limit your alcohol to one drink, don't drink at all.

4. Do not nap during the day. If you do nap, confine it to one brief nap no later than early afternoon.

If you have followed these four recommendations and are still having problems with sleep, over-the-counter melatonin at five mg may help and is very safe. If sleep still remains a problem even with melatonin, you should ask your healthcare provider if any prescription sleep medications would be safe and helpful. Some sleep medications have antidepressant activities and do not carry the risk of dependence. In my experience, good sleep hygiene (following recommendations 1–4) does not help clinically depressed people with insomnia as much as it does help insomniacs who don't have depression.

If a person snores loudly, stops breathing periodically at night, wakes up unrefreshed, and falls asleep very quickly at times they don't want to fall asleep, they may have sleep apnea syndrome, which can contribute to depression. Sleep studies can confirm the diagnosis and treatment often results in dramatic improvement.

## Eating

Undereating or overeating are common symptoms of depression. Those with poor appetites need to be encouraged to eat something healthy at least three times a day. Because of poor motivation and low energy, in addition to poor appetite, eating meals may take much longer than usual. Those with increased appetites should try to practice portion control and eliminate snacks, especially unhealthy snacks. There has been considerable research regarding healthy diets in general, less so regarding diets for depressed people. If nothing else, a healthy diet reduces your risk of heart disease and stroke and prevents or improves control of diabetes, high blood pressure, and high cholesterol.

The following is considered a healthy diet by most nutritionists:

1. The diet should be low in saturated fats and trans fats but with adequate amounts of monounsaturated or polyunsaturated fats including omega-3 fatty acids with eicosatetraenoic acid (EPA) and docosahexaenoic acid (DHA).

2. Avoid processed foods, especially refined carbohydrates and sugar (carbohydrates should mostly come from whole gains).

3. Half of your daily food intake should be from fruits and vegetables.

4. Meats should be lean—chicken and fish are especially good.

5. Tree nuts (not peanuts) and legumes (e.g., beans) should be consumed regularly.

The Mediterranean diet and the DASH diet meet many of these recommendations.

There is evolving evidence that a keto (ketogenic) diet is helpful in depression. These diets, which are high in protein and low in carbohydrates, can be found on the internet and are relatively easy to follow. At first, they often result in dramatic weight loss, so they should not be used in underweight patients or normal weight patients who are losing weight from their depressions.

There is some evidence for the helpfulness of two nutritional supplements in *augmenting* the treatment of depression, namely L-methyl folate and omega-3 fatty acids. They should *not* be used as the primary treatment. Over-the-counter L-methyl folate is a precursor of the B vitamin folic acid that helps with the production of serotonin, norepinephrine, and dopamine. Some people don't make as much L-methyl folate as others, and low levels of L-methyl folate *may* contribute to depression (please note I say *may* contribute). There is no way to test for a deficiency. L-methyl folate is very safe, so it may be worth a try for depressed people, especially if they have not completely responded to standard antidepressant treatment regimens. It is taken daily as a 15-mg pill. There is also some evidence for the effectiveness in *augmenting* the treatment of depression with the nutritional supplement omega-3 fatty acids. It *may* help in the treatment of depression. The EPA component of omega-3 should be listed on the omega-3 packaging. You should take 1,000 to 2,000 mg of EPA per day. Even at this dose it has few side effects apart from mild gastrointestinal upset, which usually resolves with use. This amount of EPA needed for treatment of depression is much greater than many over-the-counter omega-3 products contain. Again, I would not use it as primary treatment. And again, I do not believe "natural" is always better.

## Exercise

More and more research studies support the importance of exercise in preventing and treating depression. Of the three habits discussed here—sleep, diet, and exercise—exercise has the most evidence for its effectiveness. Some of the chemicals released into the brain during exercise seem to help with depression—possibly though changes in neuroplasticity. Just how much and what kind of exercise is best in depression is still being studied. Exercise intense enough to increase respiratory rate, heart rate, and/or sweating for thirty minutes a day for five days a week is probably helpful. We know that this much exercise helps prevent heart disease and strokes and prevents and improves control of diabetes, high blood pressure, and high cholesterol. Everyone with depression should regularly exercise, but poor motivation and low energy keep many from doing so. Even committing to five minutes a day is a good start. You can find many exercise regimens online for free.

## MINDFULNESS

Mindfulness alone or mindfulness with body posturing and/or exercise is receiving increased research attention in the treatment of anxiety and depression. I would not use these approaches as a primary treatment, but they may be helpful as an adjunct in some patients.

Two common mindfulness approaches are attentive breathing and attentive progressive relaxation. Taking a conscious break to breathe slowly, in and out, lowers signs of stress in your body. You need to focus your full attention on your breathing which works, in part, by distracting you from anxious thoughts. Like attentive breathing, progressively relaxing parts of your body lowers signs of stress. Start with consciously relaxing your toes, then adding your feet, then your calves, and work your way up to your scalp until your entire body is relaxed. Stay relaxed for five to fifteen minutes.

Meditation, another form of mindfulness, also lowers physical signs of stress. It is more effective for anxiety than depression, but it may help the latter. For Christians, I recommend that Jesus or some godly thought be the focus of attention—not some vague "inner self" or non-Christian spiritual focus. Christian meditation can also be a form of prayer, an inner connection with the triune God. I find I need a focus like a verse in a Psalm to help me focus.

Yoga, qigong, and tai chi seem to be helpful in ameliorating anxiety and depression. They combine mindfulness with body posturing and/or other physical components.

Historically yoga has been associated with ancient Eastern religions. Yoga focuses on postures and mindfulness with attentive breathing and meditation. If the meditation has a Christian focus, yoga does not seem to me to conflict with Christian belief and practice.

Historically, qigong has been associated with ancient Chinese philosophy. It involves "working with the life energy" in various ways. It seems to me that it would be hard to practice qigong without the embedded non-Christian philosophy.

Tai chi has its origin in the Chinese martial arts. It involves slow, graceful, focused exercise, stretching, balance, and deep breathing. With my limited knowledge of the three, yoga, qigong and tai chi, it seems to me that tai chi is the most compatible with the Christian faith.

I personally combine mindfulness with exercise by paying attention to what my body is doing during my low-impact aerobic exercise regimen for thirty minutes four days per week and by chasing away any other thoughts while I am exercising.

## CHOOSING A HEALTHCARE PROVIDER

It is important to choose the right healthcare provider to help you with the medical aspects of treating depression. There are many who can help you with these medical aspects, including psychiatrists, primary care physicians, psychiatric nurse practitioners, primary care nurse practitioners, and primary care physician assistants. You should feel confident that your healthcare provider really listens to you and genuinely cares about your suffering. You need to be able to trust and have confidence in him/her. If you don't, you are less likely to be healed from your depression.

Many healthcare providers are good with brief counseling techniques, but many depressed people can benefit from more in-depth counseling. Psychiatrists and psychiatric nurse practitioners are trained in in-depth counseling, but most healthcare insurances don't pay them well for it, so they may not offer it. Many trained counselors have a fairly good knowledge base regarding psychiatric medications, but they cannot prescribe them. The better counselors will know when referral for possible medical treatment is in order. They usually appropriately recommend continued counseling while receiving medical treatment. Some counselors have a bias against medication, a bias that I believe is not justified. If you are suffering from a moderate depression and especially a moderately severe depression or a severe depression, at least consider medications. The large majority of healthcare providers will not pressure you into taking medication if you don't want to. They do, however, want you to know what your medical options are and the hope for healing they can bring.

# 7

## Psychosocial Causes, Contributors, and Triggers of Depression

THE PSYCHOSOCIAL ASPECTS OF depression relate to the immaterial aspect of our being, as discussed in chapter 2. I believe that the word *psychosocial* is more inclusive than psychological, as it recognizes the social dimension of our being. There are many psychosocial causes, contributors, and triggers of depression. Although I sometimes use these words interchangeably, there are nuanced differences. *Cause* can imply that one factor is the main culprit in the etiology of the depression. Sometimes there is a main factor in depression, but uncommonly there is only one factor. *Contributor* implies that there are multiple factors at work in the etiology of a depression. Usually there are multiple factors at work. *Trigger* implies that one situation is the immediate precipitator of the depression. Though a trigger might be quickly identified, it is commonly not the only issue that needs to be addressed.

As we have said, there are many psychosocial causes, contributors, and triggers of depression. I will briefly address only some of the most common ones. There are many excellent Christian books that address the psychosocial aspect of depression in greater detail. I particularly recommend *When Life Goes Dark* and *Light in the Darkness* (see Selective Bibliography).

## ROOTS IN CHILDHOOD

### Parental Influences

Victims of childhood trauma are often predisposed to depression. In one recent study of individuals with depression, 46 percent reported childhood mistreatment. Physical abuse and sexual abuse are obvious contributors, but verbal and emotional abuse, neglect, and rejection can also factor in. Parents who reject or ignore their children can leave them with lasting wounds. An unloved child often experiences marked loss of self-esteem and self-worth, which can contribute to depression in childhood or later in life. Sadly, the psychological defenses these abused, neglected, and rejected children used to protect their fragile egos in childhood may hurt them in adulthood. The old rules of engagement can sabotage present-day relationships. Other common contributors in childhood to later depression are mental illness in a parent, domestic violence, parental separation or divorce, substance abuse, or a caregiver with a criminal history. Many victims of childhood maltreatment score positive on the PHQ-9 question 6: "[Have you been] feeling bad about yourself or that you are a failure or have let yourself or your family down?"

Many dysfunctional parenting styles can contribute to loss of self-esteem and self-worth in children. Children in status-seeking families and/or families with unrealistically high or rigid standards are predisposed to depression. The children often feel pressured to meet their parents' expectations, and failure to meet those expectations often negatively affects them. These children may become excessively demanding of themselves in later life, even perfectionistic, contributing to depression from a form of burnout. Those with perfectionistic tendencies are often unable to accept without guilt or shame their own mistakes, and they have difficulty adjusting to life's setbacks. They have trouble believing that God accepts them just as they are, with their imperfections. Legalistic Christianity with its long lists of do's and don'ts opens up endless opportunities for failure. Some "shoulds" are needed in life, but too many shoulds can rob faith of its joy. Many perfectionists are also workaholics and really should (this should is an exception) include more leisure in their lives.

Overly critical parents can lead to self-critical children who can become depressed when young or later in life. I'm not suggesting parents should ignore negative behavior, only that they should not undermine their children in the process of disciplining them. Fortunately, another caring person, such as a grandmother, aunt, or even a caring sibling, can reduce the negative impact of dysfunctional parents.

## Temperamental Predisposition and Attachment

The parents of depressed children can be model parents. The parents aren't the only factor in predisposing to depression. Infants and young children bring their own temperaments into the parent-child relationship. Some infants and young children are "easy" to nurture, while some are "difficult." How the mother and child interact with each other, how they attach, can result in a "secure" attachment or an "insecure" attachment. Later in life these children often have relationship styles with other people that mirror their previous mother-child relationship. Some insecure attachments can lead to relationship styles that predispose to depression in later childhood and adult life. One major branch of counseling addresses problematic relationships—interpersonal therapy (IPT)—more on this in chapter 9. Many relationship styles that contribute to depression start at a very young age and may require a long time and much effort to change in counseling.

## CURRENT CIRCUMSTANCES

Fear may contribute to depression. An abusive spouse or living in violent neighborhoods may be contributors to depression, or even trigger it. Sometimes the fear-producing event is so intense that it can lead to post-traumatic stress disorder (PTSD), which predisposes one to depressive episodes.

The social environment we live in may contribute to depression. Being trapped in excessively demanding or meaningless jobs or excessive caretaker responsibilities (e.g., with disabled children or frail parents) can lead to depression.

Poverty is a common cause of depression. There is often a spiral downward because of the relationship between poverty and depression. The disability of depression can lead to unemployment and the resulting poverty can lead to depression. Long-term unemployed people are three times more likely to become depressed.

Minorities are disproportionately affected by depression. This may have to do with prejudice, lack of opportunities, and a sense of not being accepted by the majority of the population.

Some depressed people suffer, in part, from learned helplessness. They believe that, no matter how hard they try, nothing will relieve their suffering. They feel helpless and easily give up. Often this attitude and approach to life begins in childhood. They may have lived in a dysfunctional family where they really were helpless. People with learned helplessness feel as if they have no control over the things they want to be different. Part of the problem may be that they try to gain control over things they can't control and do not take control of things they can. This is a common problem in older depressed people, who feel as if the important parts of their lives are over and that their physical and mental capacities are diminishing.

Social isolation often leads to depression. More Americans are living alone today than at any other time in our history. Social isolation can also be the result of depression. Withdrawing from others physically or even emotionally can deepen one's depression.

Financial difficulties can lead to depression. Wondering whether you can pay the monthly bills is very stressful. In some studies, financial problems are as likely to contribute to depression as divorce.

Intense and/or prolonged stress of any kind can lead to depression. The COVID-19 pandemic, occurring at the time this book was written, has been very stressful for many people, especially those who are depressed. The social isolation, fear, and financial pressures the pandemic have created can contribute to an ongoing depression and sometimes trigger new depression in vulnerable people.

Common things like a car wreck or losing an important computer file or your roof leaking can be very stressful. Often depression is precipitated by the effect of multiple stressors coming together all at once in a perfect storm. Each of the stressors alone might have been coped with, but not the simultaneous occurrence of more than one.

It may be that the mental energy required in daily life in modern America predisposes us to depression. Most of our lives are filled with daily activities that require a level of mental energy that a century ago wasn't needed. Just think about when you last went grocery shopping. How many choices did you have to make? Do I need ketchup? If so, which of many brands should I buy? Am I looking for quality or price? Do I need salad dressing? If so, which of many brands should I buy? Am I looking for quality or price? Do I need meat? Etc., etc. When I am depressed, I find shopping terribly draining. I can't wait to get back home. And when you surf the internet or interact with others on the internet, how rapidly do you go from one screen to another? How many times do you click your mouse in one sitting? How often do you have really meaningful conversations on the internet? And shopping and the internet are only two of numerous things requiring a lot mental energy that we experience every day in modern society.

Blurred boundaries can dramatically increase stress leading to depression from burnout. Some people find it hard to say no to new or increased responsibilities. They may even know that they are already doing too much, but they fear disappointing people. They may believe that sacrificial living requires them to deny their own needs and legitimate desires.

The idea of *margins* is helpful in setting appropriate boundaries (see *Margins: Restoring Emotional, Physical, Financial, and Time Reserves to Overloaded Lives* by Richard Swenson, MD). Think of your day as a written page in a book. Write in your plans for the day with adequate margins so that when something unexpected comes up, you can write that new responsibility in the margins, not squeezed in between the lines. If you do not have adequate margins, you are always under pressure to keep up with the day's demands; your day can easily become overwhelming. Adequate margins also make it easier for you to respond to unplanned opportunities to be Christ's servant to those he puts in your path. When no unplanned opportunities surface, those margins can also be places to rest and reflect during the day. These times of rest and reflection are definitely not wasted time.

Psychosocial causes, contributors, and triggers abound in our daily lives as Americans. Some come as part of our lives that we can't control and we should not focus on them. We can control, at least in part, some parts of our lives. If we have tried and have trouble coping with our stresses, we should seek help from a counselor.

# 8

## Distressing Feelings Associated with Depression

MANY DISTRESSING FEELINGS ARE commonly associated with depression. It is not always clear whether the feelings contribute to the cause of depression or are the effects of depression, or both. Regardless, they need to be addressed.

Some Christians believe that feelings shouldn't be trusted. In their way of thinking, feelings are more susceptible than thoughts to the influence of sin. However, if the feeling of "tormented despair" is to be distrusted, shouldn't the feeling of "surprising joy" be distrusted as well?

Feelings are very real and should be acknowledged as an important part of our lives; the biblical psalmist did so, as did many other biblical authors. Feelings should not be ignored or vilified. Merely validating a depressed person's feelings often brings some relief. Also helpful to depressed people is knowing that others have experienced the brokenness of depression, have walked through the darkness, and recovered. I have seen this positive effect repeatedly in our depression support group.

While a painful feeling is very real and should be acknowledged, it is important to look for an *inaccurate negative thought* behind a feeling. If there is a negative thought present and if it is not accurate, truthful alternative thoughts need to be uncovered. Once such an untruth is discovered, depressed people need to regularly remind themselves of the truthful alternative thought. This is one of the main principles behind one major approach to counseling—cognitive-behavioral therapy (CBT). More on this in chapter 9.

Unlike some CBT counselors, however, I believe that the distressing feelings associated with depression are often not due to negative thoughts but are a direct result of the brain's neurochemical and neuroelectric dysfunction. One of many pieces of evidence that the thought behind a feeling is not always the cause of the feeling is the fact that, in terms of the severity of feelings associated with depression, morning is usually much worse than later in the day. It is not that we think more negative thoughts in the morning, leading to more distressing feelings. Rather, the circadian rhythm of our brains influences our mood through neurochemical and neuroelectric changes. My own experience with depressive feelings in the morning is that I often see no reason at all for my feelings. There are no negative thoughts that precede the feeling. In fact, the negative feelings precede the thoughts. The feelings are just a part of the illness of depression, not some dysfunction of thoughts. Another example that a negative thought does not always precede a distressing feeling is premenstrual dysphoric disorder, where the negative feelings only surface before monthly menstruation with its hormonal changes. Fortunately, more and more CBT counselors are directly addressing feelings as well as thoughts.

We will address six categories of distressing feelings: loneliness and abandonment; failure and worthlessness; anger and unforgiveness; guilt and shame; anxiety and fear; and grief and loss. All of these feelings may contribute to depression, result from depression, or both. We will not deal with the distressing feelings of despair and hopelessness in this chapter. They are addressed in many parts of this book. Despair and hopelessness were especially addressed in a literary fashion in chapter 2 and they will be especially focused on again in chapter 13.

## LONELINESS AND ABANDONMENT

Depressed people often feel lonely. I have a good friend whose chief external cause of depression is loneliness, partly because of a divorce four years ago. Loneliness is a feeling of inner emptiness with a sense of isolation. Most people have a deep desire to closely relate to at least one other person—a need to be loved and to love another person. The loneliness a depressed person feels has a more painful quality to it than loneliness experienced by others. People without a close friend are much more likely to become depressed when severely stressed than those who have a close friend. I recommend that you nurture at least two close friendships so that if one dies, or the relationship is otherwise severed, you are not left completely bereft. However, some people feel lonely even if they have many friends and loneliness may be present even when involved with others socially.

Some people do not have a much-needed social support system to keep them from becoming depressed or to help them cope with and recover from depression. For Christians, their church fellowship can be a major part of their social support system. Research shows that overall, those involved in faith communities are less lonely. Sadly, some Christians do not take advantage of this support system. Sadder yet are churches that are not welcoming, caring, or proactively reaching out to depressed people.

Hebrews 10:24–25 says, "Let us consider how to stir up one another to love and good works, not neglecting to meet together, as is the habit of some, but encouraging one another." Depressed people need to try to participate in some church activities, to *meet together*, even though it may be challenging. Church attendance can be *encouraging* to depressed people. At first, they may wisely choose to come late to a worship service and leave early so they don't have overwhelming interactions with many other people. But just being among others of like faith can help bring some relief from depression. That has been the case with me.

For those suffering from depression, getting out of an empty house to spend time with caring people, either individually or in groups, can be very difficult. The anxiety related to social engagement and the poor motivation and low energy of depression are major obstacles for them. But just "doing it"—just getting out—can be helpful. Volunteering in a low-pressure activity for short periods of time on a regular basis can be helpful.

In our depression support group, I do not require anyone to actively participate; listening is just fine. I tell new members that if another person or I asks someone a question, they may say something like "I don't know how to answer that" or "I'm not sure about that." There's no need to feel ashamed if you are quiet and reserved in group settings. If you try to get out but just can't quite do it, or if you need to leave a gathering early, don't take on inappropriate guilt. You have tried, and that is good enough for today. But do try again tomorrow.

Depressed Christians can be reassured that they are never alone, much less completely abandoned. Often, however, depressed Christians do feel abandoned by God. This feeling is incongruent with what the Bible teaches. Moses said to Joshua on the verge of taking possession of the promised land, "It is the Lord who goes before you. He will be with you; he will not leave you or forsake you. Do not fear or be dismayed" (Deuteronomy 31:8). With the many challenges depressed people face each day, this is a good verse to remember. Many of the Scripture verses in this and other sections of this book can be found in Appendix C. You may want to cut out particularly helpful verses and tape them to your bathroom mirror.

Although many depressed people suffer from feeling abandoned by God, those previously abandoned by a parent or spouse often suffer the most. This earthly abandonment makes them especially vulnerable to fear and despair that their heavenly Father and divine Beloved has abandoned them. They may need to be reminded over and over again in a sensitive way that God is always with them.

The following is the first of fourteen prayers you can pray with Laurelle Moody, each found after a relevant section of this book. I met Laurelle when she was about four years old, riding her rocking horse in the home of a now close friend of forty years. For years, Laurelle has experienced the physical and mental suffering of chronic Lyme disease. She has recently started to really improve and is willing to share the kinds of prayers that helped sustain her. Laurelle wrote each prayer specifically for each section. You can find all fourteen of her prayers in Appendix D. You may want to pray a different prayer every morning on a biweekly cycle.

> *My Lord, who sticks closer than a brother, I feel so lonely! It seems like you have abandoned me in this place of barren emptiness. I cry out to you and hear no reply. It feels like no one knows or understands me or my pain. Yet I realize, Jesus, that you know and understand. You were a man of sorrows who experienced utter abandonment—total aloneness. Though I feel hollow inside, I know that your Holy Spirit lives within me. Please help me to believe that you never leave or forsake me.*
>
> *I ask you to give me wisdom to make good choices so that I don't isolate myself from the very people you are calling to walk with me and provide uplifting support. When I know I should connect with others but don't have it in me to take the necessary steps, please become my motivation and inspiration.*
>
> *Thank you for making me part of your family. You created us to need each other. Still, I know relationships can be hard. Let me find comfort in knowing that when others fail me or I fail others, you are always faithful. Thank you for being my Constant Companion.*

## FAILURE AND WORTHLESSNESS

Depressed people often feel that they are failures and/or worthless. They don't see setbacks as "failings"; they see themselves as "being a failure."

Healthy minds recognize that failings can help them learn from their mistakes and help them change their future. If the future can't be changed in some areas of their lives, mentally healthy people learn how to live with their weaknesses and capitalize on their strengths.

Depressed people often think of themselves as failures that God could never use—worthless in his eyes. They may need to be reminded that God never, ever thinks of us as failures or being worthless, even when we fail, even when we make mistakes, even when we sin. The Bible tells us that we are all highly valued by God in spite of our perceived or real failings (more on this in chapter 12). The loving earthly father eagerly waited for, ran to, enrobed, and prepared a feast for the wayward prodigal son (Luke 15). Our Father in heaven does the same for all of us when we fail or sin.

Here are what two biblical authors had to say about our worth in God's eyes: The most beloved king of Israel, King David, says in Psalm 139:13–14, "You formed my inward most parts; you knitted me together in my mother's womb. I praise you, for I am fearfully and wonderfully made. Wonderful are your works." Say to yourself, "I am wonderful because you made me wonderful." In Psalm 8:3–5, King David says, "When I look at your heavens, the work of your fingers, the moon and the stars, which you have set in place, what is man that you are mindful of him, and the son of man that you care for him? Yet you have made him a little lower than the heavenly beings and crowned him with glory and honor." What has God done for you? He has crowned with glory and honor. You are of great worth in God's eyes. The Apostle Paul in Ephesians 2:10 says to those who have been saved through faith by grace, "We are his workmanship, created in Christ Jesus for good works." In fact, you are Christ Jesus' workmanship even without the good works that non-depressed Christians seem to effortlessly do.

Commonly in decades past, when some of us were young, recognizing self-worth and cultivating self-esteem was frowned on in Christian circles. Many equated self-worth with arrogance and self-esteem with self-centeredness. Taken to the extreme, self-worth and self-esteem can indeed be a rationalization for sinful pride. But drawing one's self-worth and self-esteem from a knowledge of how God views us is not arrogant. God's view of our worth needs to become our view of our worth. That he died on the cross for us is dramatic evidence of our worth in his sight.

Often depressed people think others view them as failures or worthless. Though there are exceptions, this is usually not true of the people whose opinions should really matter to us. Since so many people are depressed or know someone who is depressed, it is likely that at least some people you interact with will be sympathetic—not judgmental.

*My Creator, who formed me with infinite wisdom and tender care, it is hard to come to you right now. It seems like everything I do falls short, and I don't measure up . . . My weaknesses, flaws, and inabilities make me feel like such a failure! Between my shortcomings and my sins, I imagine that you shake your head in disgust. Yet your Word says that isn't true. Even when I fail, you run to embrace me whenever I turn to you! Jesus, thank you for dying on the cross and securing my forgiveness. You must treasure me more than I can comprehend to pay such a high price!*

*Still, I wrestle with a deep sense of worthlessness. Please remind me that my worth is not wrapped up in my performance. It is so easy to rely on my own negative thoughts, feelings, and evaluations when defining myself. But you say that I am a whole new creation in Christ Jesus—designed to do good works! Strengthen my faith. Help me believe that you can take my imperfect offerings and use them in meaningful ways. Thank you for redeeming my failures and investing so much to prove how deeply you value me.*

## ANGER AND UNFORGIVENESS

The following on anger and unforgiveness is, in part, a reflection on the topic as presented in Dr. Richard Winter's book *When Life Goes Dark* (see Selective Bibliography). There are three reasons I sometimes defer to Winter's discussion in my book. First, his book is very helpful to those who care for depressed people; I want to commend Dr. Winter's material. Second, I have little personal experience with anger. I am one of those rare people who hardly ever gets angry. When I do get angry, it usually resolves in a few minutes. I do not think of this as a virtue, as I don't have to discipline myself to avoid angry feelings and unforgiveness. If fact, there have been times when I should have gotten angry and didn't. Third, I rarely address anger in the context of brief counseling in my medical office. If it comes up (uncommonly), it requires too much time for me to properly address in the short time I have with family medicine patients. I almost always refer people having trouble controlling their anger to a counselor, including trained clergy.

Anger is *not* always an *in*appropriate feeling. God gets angry, but his anger is always righteous anger. God hates sin, evil, and injustice, and it causes him to be angry. To think of God as capable of anger is offensive to many modern people, even some Christians, but it is a great comfort to those who are or have been the victims of sin, evil, and/or injustice. The Apostle John reported that when Jesus found his friend, Lazarus, dead, "he was deeply moved in his spirit and greatly troubled" (John 11:33; see also

v. 38). The literal Greek meaning of the phrase "deeply moved" is "snorted like a horse with anger." In this situation, Jesus' anger was directed at the brokenness of the world as manifested in Lazarus's death. Death was not a part of God's original plan for creation. God gets angry when we sin, but he does not get angry at us because of our brokenness (more on this in chapter 12). Thankfully, the Bible says that God is "slow to anger" (Exodus 34:6) and "his anger is but for a moment" (Psalm 30:5).

Our anger may be appropriate, or it may be inappropriate. Paul says, "Be angry and do not sin" (Ephesians 4:26). That means that not all anger is sin. We need to reflect on what we are angry about and how our anger is expressed to determine whether there is a sinful component to our anger. We should ask questions of ourselves such as "Am I angry because I want to hurt the person who caused my hurt or am I angry to stimulate positive change in that person?" Also, "Is the degree of my anger proportional to the inciting situation?" Another related question is, "Does my anger want to diminish the effects of sin, evil, and/or injustice or tear down the sinner, the evil person, or the unjust person?" We need to be intolerant of sin, evil, and injustice, but we should remember that sinful, evil, and unjust people are still loved by God and should be loved by us as well. If, in our anger, we have sinned, God is quick to forgive us if we confess our sin, repent, and make amends.

It usually requires wisdom to know when expressing our anger is appropriate or inappropriate. Depressed people often have a harder time controlling their anger—which is often disproportionate to the inciting situation. We need to take that into account when we are one of the people on the receiving end of the depressed person's anger. We should try not to take the anger personally. This does not mean the anger shouldn't be addressed. It should be addressed, but in an understanding and kind way, not repaying anger with anger.

Often anger is a secondary reaction, a result of feeling emotionally hurt, guilt-ridden, fearful, or merely frustrated. Addressing the underlying hurt, guilt, fear, or frustration may be more productive than directly addressing the anger itself.

Those who bottle up their anger are also vulnerable to depression. They often suppress their anger to avoid uncomfortable conflict with others. Unresolved anger can lead to bitterness and resentment, which can contribute to depression.

> *My Prince of Peace, there are times when I'm overtaken by anger.*
> *It can flare up at the smallest irritation—consuming my emotions*
> *and enflaming my reactions. I don't want to be ruled by anger . . .*

*feeling on edge and out of control. Instead, I want the inner calm and self-control that your Spirit brings. Give me discernment to know when my anger is righteous and when it is not. Reign in my life so that anger won't lead me to sin.*

*When anger begins to arise, I want to remember you and call out for help. If there is some underlying factor behind my anger, I ask you to reveal it and guide me as I seek to address the problem in a healthy way. When I'm mistreated and want to respond with retaliation and revenge, please restrain that urge. If I'm struggling to forgive, help me to keep asking you to fill me with your love and forgiveness toward those who have wronged me. If I need to take further steps to resolve conflict with someone, enable me to move forward in your grace, strength, and wisdom. Thank you that I can lean on you to defuse my anger and replace it with your peace.*

## GUILT AND SHAME

The feeling of guilt is an important part of our mental and spiritual health. Guilt is that distressing feeling associated with regret, remorse, and/or self-condemnation that comes from wrong thoughts, words, or actions. Guilt can helpfully prompt us to repent and make amends when we have thought wickedly, spoken foolishly, or done wrong. And it can keep us from doing the same wrong thing again. Even some secular psychological research has shown that appropriate guilt has a positive impact on mental health. Despite this, the importance of the conscience has been eroded by much modern and even more by postmodern thinking.

The conscience is the "organ" that helps us recognize right from wrong. It makes us feel guilty when we do wrong, and makes us feel good, but not self-righteous, when we do right. A pure, healthy conscience is something to be desired and pursued. Early in many Christian lives, godly parents and influential people in the church help us (or should help us) develop a healthy conscience—what the Bible sometimes calls a "pure heart." As we grow older, our consciences can become more and more pure or more and more "defiled" (Titus 1:15: "To the pure, all things are pure, but to the defiled and unbelieving, nothing is pure; but both their minds and their consciences are defiled"). Using the word *defiled*, Paul means that truthful standards of right and wrong can become distorted; we become unable to sense the pollution of our consciences with impure thoughts.

Even healthy consciences are imperfect and tainted by sin and need to be shaped and reshaped by God's Word. Through lack of proper use, our hearts can become hardened. The prophet Ezekiel reports what God said to Israel regarding the restoration of their promised land after the Babylonian exile: "If they will set aside their detestable things . . . I will remove the heart of stone from their flesh and give them a heart of flesh, that they may walk in my statutes and keep my rules and obey them. And they shall be my people, and I will be their God" (Ezekiel 11:18–20). Our hearts need to be softened by God—"the heart of stone" replaced with "a heart of flesh," so that God's gracious laws, designed for our good, shape and reshape our minds, and so that we "walk in [God's] statutes." Thankfully, God empowers us through the Holy Spirit to follow his life-giving rules and be happily obedient to him.

When I go for a period of time without having a guilty feeling, it is usually because my heart has been hardened to the many small, and sometimes large, disobediences in my thoughts, words, or deeds. Little, and sometimes bigger, sins of omission and commission have gone unnoticed by me. I have become nearly dead spiritually, and I need the Holy Spirit to quicken my heart. Once I am made aware of my sin, I usually quickly confess my sin and then appropriately put the guilt behind me, knowing that Jesus is interceding for me at the *throne of grace*—what past Christian generations called the *mercy seat*. Jesus' death on the cross for my sin and his resurrection assures me that I am no longer guilty. This is how I deal with guilt when I am not depressed.

When I am depressed, everything is different. Even small things weigh heavily on my conscience, and I repeatedly confess my sins with no sense of God's full forgiveness. I repeatedly ask myself, "Am I truly forgiven?" Many of the things I feel guilty about are not "sins" at all (more on this in chapter 11). Worse, I feel guilty for being depressed. I even know some depressed people who feel guilty about feeling guilty for feeling depressed. These people and I are not helped by those who place a strong emphasis on sin as the cause of depression. Many of us who are depressed are all too quick to take on additional inappropriate guilt when we are depressed.

The tender, fragile consciences of some depressed people are burdened with inappropriate guilty feelings, sometimes called false guilt. I don't like the term *false guilt* because the guilt feels very real. The vulnerability to *inappropriate guilt* is often shaped in childhood and adolescence. For example, people who have grown up in a family where they have been constantly criticized often develop perfectionist standards. This perfectionism can lead to inappropriate guilt from a sense of failure to meet unrealistic, unobtainable, perfectionist goals.

The Bible says that when we are truly guilty because of sin, we need to confess our sin and repent (change direction) and make amends. Then we need to try to immediately dispel our guilt. It may be hard for people to put away guilt that is no longer appropriate. This is especially the case in depression, when guilt can become an obsession. The depressed person may believe that he/she is too bad for God to forgive him/her. This person must be gently challenged in regards to this belief. To remain guilt-ridden is in a sense a denial that our God, in Jesus Christ, has done what he said he has done, namely, forgiven the sins of all who trust him, including our own sins. Of course, if a depressed person has tried to dispel guilt and still has guilty feelings, he/she should not feel guilty about feeling guilty.

If *guilt* is about feeling bad because of what we have *done*, *shame* is about who we feel we *are*. When we have done something bad, we should feel guilty until we have repented, but with shame we believe and feel like a bad person that cannot change. Paul says in 2 Corinthians 7:10, "Godly grief produces repentance that leads to salvation without regret, whereas worldly grief produces death." Surely shame must be one example of worldly grief—it is a sort of death to the soul. Shame is a deeply troubling feeling of disgrace that makes one believe and feel like a fundamentally bad person—a shameful person. Some of my thoughts on shame come from the well-written book *The Soul of Shame,* by the Christian psychiatrist Curt Thompson.

The neural circuits in the brain giving us a sense of shame may begin as early as fifteen months of age, and once those circuits are laid down, they are hard to change. The way parents respond to an infant's distress, including nonverbal communication, can result in shame-filled patterns of response in later life. When there are more wounds and barbs throughout life it can lead to further shame. Shame almost always comes in response to someone treating us as though we deserve shame. Even a raised eyebrow can trigger the neural circuits of shame. And the mental energy we use to keep others from knowing how shameful we are can contribute to depression.

I have found in depression support groups that the sharing of the things we are ashamed of only comes after many sessions with people who have listened to us and have become trustworthy in responding compassionately. We are so ashamed of ourselves that we believe others will believe we are shameful people. When we are bold enough to share what we believe is our worst with trustworthy people, healing often begins. Depressed people are often so good at hiding their shame that I often ask them, one on one, whether they feel ashamed. They may at first deny it—they may not even recognize they have it at first—but it opens the door for them to come back to me when they trust me enough with their shame-filled story. With enough time, resisting believing our untrue story of shame can lead to a different true story of new creation in Jesus Christ.

Often people who have been the victim of sin feel ashamed. Physical or sexual abuse and/or verbal or emotional abuse or neglect can cause shame at the time of the abuse or neglect, and again later in life. This feeling of shame is worse for depressed people and harder for them to overcome.

Shame often causes feelings of worthlessness that come from failing to live up to someone's expectations—our own or other people's or God's expectations. The shame resulting from this perceived or real failure can be hard to endure. Those with shame often misperceive God's expectation regarding themselves. They may believe that God is too demanding; they cannot meet his demands. However, Jesus says, "My yoke is easy, my burden is light" (Matthew 11:30). God does make demands on us, but they are not onerous; they are easy and light. They are certainly easier and lighter than the burden of inappropriate shame.

Even secular psychological research studies have shown that appropriate *guilt* dealt with promptly is associated with positive moods and good relationships, while *shame* leads to self-destructive thoughts, feelings, and behaviors and dysfunctional relationships. If you feel ashamed, pray fervently that God will remove this terribly hurtful inappropriate feeling. Jesus will not leave you or forsake you when you share your story with him. He already knows your story and loves you deeply in spite of it. He does not believe the lie that you are a shameful person. He wants to bring about a much better story for you.

> *My Loving Father, these constant feelings of guilt and shame make me want to hide and shrink from your presence. Will I ever be free of this heavy self-condemnation? Will I ever feel forgiven and clean? How I yearn for acceptance! Jesus, remind me of the good news that your death and resurrection won for me the divine forgiveness and acceptance that I crave! Because of your victory, I can be assured of your warm, approving smile. Thank you for always wanting me to come to you—no matter my condition!*
>
> *Please develop a pure, healthy conscience within me and empower me to walk in your ways. When I feel guilty because of sin, let it lead to confession and repentance. I ask you to liberate me from any lingering feelings of inappropriate guilt. If I'm assaulted by lies that define me as a bad person, bring to mind my new identity in you, Jesus. When shame persists in pointing its boney finger, I'm tempted to cover myself with "good" achievements . . . frantically trying to quiet the harsh accusations. Still, all my striving doesn't work. In these moments, help me look to you in childlike faith—trusting that your yoke is easy and your burden is light. This is possible because you perfectly fulfilled the righteous demands and expectations expressed in your law . . . and you did it on my behalf! May this reality provide relief and rest.*

*I trust that one day you will bring healing so that my feelings will align with your truth. But until then, steady me with deep confidence in knowing that you don't condemn me for these feelings. Thank you for understanding how hard and painful they are . . . and for the compassion in your eyes.*

## ANXIETY AND FEAR

Anxiety is such a broad topic that we can discuss it only briefly. Mild anxiety is often helpful when there is a realistic concern that needs to be addressed. It motivates the anxious person to do what needs to be done. However, Jesus speaks to unnecessary anxiety in life in Matthew 6:25–34:

> 25 "Therefore I tell you, do not be anxious about your life, what you will eat or what you will drink, nor about your body, what you will put on. Is not life more than food, and the body more than clothing? 26 Look at the birds of the air: they neither sow nor reap nor gather into barns, and yet your heavenly Father feeds them. Are you not of more value than they? 27 And which of you by being anxious can add a single hour to his span of life? 28 And why are you anxious about clothing? Consider the lilies of the field, how they grow: they neither toil nor spin, 29 yet I tell you, even Solomon in all his glory was not arrayed like one of these. 30 But if God so clothes the grass of the field, which today is alive and tomorrow is thrown into the oven, will he not much more clothe you, O you of little faith? 31 Therefore do not be anxious, saying, 'What shall we eat?' or 'What shall we drink?' or 'What shall we wear?' 32 For the Gentiles seek after all these things, and your heavenly Father knows that you need them all. 33 But seek first the kingdom of God and his righteousness, and all these things will be added to you. 34 "Therefore do not be anxious about tomorrow, for tomorrow will be anxious for itself. Sufficient for the day is its own trouble.

Jesus does not want us fretting and unnecessarily worrying about daily activities, such as food, drink, and clothing (Matthew 6:25–31) "for your heavenly Father knows you need them all" (v. 32) and will provide for them. We need to try to focus on the kingdom of God and leave the daily needs of this life to God. Nor should we worry about the future (vv. 33–34). God knows the beginning from the end and is actively bringing about his purposes in, for, and through us. Peter exhorts the flock of God to cast "all your anxieties on him [Jesus the chief shepherd], because he cares for you" (1 Peter 5:7).

All Christians should regularly take their anxieties to Jesus in prayer. But for many depressed anxious people, this does not resolve worries or even lessen them. These already troubled souls should not feel guilty about their persistent worries; they have tried to trust their heavenly Father and cast their anxieties on Jesus. Many depressed people simply cannot stop or control their worry. It is a part of their depression. Remind yourself, however, that your heavenly Father knows your needs and will provide for them and that Jesus cares for you now and will do so in the future. Paul encourages those who are anxious to share their anxiety with God through prayer. The promise, Paul says, is that "the peace of God, which surpasses all understanding, will guard your hearts and your minds in Christ Jesus" (Philippians 4:7). God's peace, unsurpassed divine peace, is always at work guarding us (a military term) against anxiety. But in this broken world, depressed people often do not feel this peace. They may experience uncontrolled anxiety. Thankfully, none of God's promises ever fail. Someday, maybe not until the next world, this surpassing all understanding peace will be felt in every believer's heart and mind.

Sometimes depressed people turn to short-term reliefs from anxiety. One example is alcohol or drug use. Some people avoid conflictual, but important, relationships rather than dealing with the conflict by using alcohol or drugs. A second example of short-term relief is avoiding growth-producing challenges because of a fear of failure. Short-term strategies like these avoidances, however, are not constructive. In fact, they are often destructive, keeping the fearful person from important growth in character.

Sometimes the anxiety is so intense in depression that it causes fear, even terror. The feeling is similar to what a normal person would feel if threatened by someone with a gun. Sometimes a depressed person's fear is so sudden and severe that it is called a panic attack, which we have discussed earlier.

I've known well-meaning Christians who quote to a fearful person a phrase from 1 John 4:18: "perfect love casts out fear." The implication is that fearful people do not know the love of God as they should, namely perfectly, which, by the way, none of us can. The context of this phrase, however, makes it clear that it is fear of God's final judgment that perfect love casts out. "By this [abiding in God and God abiding in us] is love perfected with us, so that we may have confidence for *the day of judgment*, because as he is, so also are we in this world. There is no fear in love, but perfect love casts out fear. For fear has to do with *punishment*, and whoever fears has not been perfected in love" (vv. 17–18, emphasis added). In my many years of caring for depressed people, rarely has the fear of the day of judgment been their chief concern. In fact, many seriously depressed people look forward to dying, and many fearful depressed Christians are not afraid of the final judgment, because they know Jesus, their mediator and advocate, will be sitting on the judgment seat dispensing mercy.

King David encourages all his people to "Be strong, and let your heart take courage, all you who wait for the Lord" (Psalm 31:24). I recommend that all fearful, depressed people try to be courageous. Courage is not the absence of fear. Rather, it is thinking what needs to be thought and doing what needs to be done to address depression in spite of fear. I also recommend trying to reframe any frightening obstacle as a challenge. A challenge may be easier to address than a frightening obstacle—though both are especially hard for depressed people.

In depressed people, rejection is one of the most common fears. We all desire the approval of others. This is not always a bad thing if we seek the approval of wise people. But it takes a negative turn when our desire for approval becomes a need for approval. We become anxious that many of the things we say or do will put us in a bad light with others. The constant worry generated by this need for approval can be both a cause and effect of depression.

> *My Good Shepherd, I'm tied up in anxious knots and frozen with fear. I can't stop my mind from racing to the worst-case scenario all the time! My thoughts are constantly pulled in a direction that grips my heart with fear—which closes in around me like a prison. Please quiet my mind and enable me to take a deep breath. I want to live in the moment . . . not worrying about the past or fretting about the future. You are here with me right now. Help me to fix my eyes on you, your provision, and your protection.*
>
> *Anxiety is such an exhausting burden. I'm frustrated because even if I place my cares in your hands, I often take them back again! I long to be free of these worries, but I'm not. Thank you for sympathizing with me and not judging. Though it is a wearying struggle, I know that you are fighting with and for me. I want to cooperate with you by filling my mind with your truth. Fortify me to faithfully spend time in your Word, in prayer, in worship, and with other believers. Even when I'm experiencing anxiety and fear, I know you are walking through this with me. Thank you!*

## GRIEF AND LOSS

So much has been written on grief that I will address it only briefly. Grief brings waves of sadness and psychological pain alternating with waves of relief—occasionally happiness, sometimes even laughter, especially if the deceased is a Christian and known to be in heaven with Jesus. At times a profound sense of loss or emptiness feels as if part of you has been ripped out. Floods of anxiety may overwhelm you at times. Brief glimpses of the beloved in another room or the imagined sound of that person's voice is not unusual. Many other symptoms of mild to moderate depression are present and normal in grief.

Most symptoms of grief begin to improve spontaneously after two to four months. If the symptoms of grief are not improving after four months—earlier if there is significant agitation, severe sleep disturbance, pervasive loss of interest in normal activities, excessive guilt, loss of self-esteem, or suicidality—the grief should be treated as clinical depression in addition to grief.

Significant losses other than a beloved's death may cause depression. In fact, loss of some sort is at least part of the cause of most depressions. There are multiple *losses* in divorce, including the hope for a happy marriage, intimate companionship, shared parenting, and shared financial security. Divorce can be harder to come to terms with than the death of a spouse. Many other losses prompt a form of grief: *loss* of a good job, *loss* of a longed-for opportunity, *loss* of a good reputation (humiliation is a particularly distressing cause of depression that I have felt—humiliation from a personal failure)—*loss* of health or physical stamina, *loss* of financial stability (another common cause of depression), and *loss* of a close friendship, to name a few. Again, if the symptoms like those of mild to moderate depression do not begin to resolve in two to four months, the depression should be treated—earlier if symptoms are like moderately severe or severe depression.

> *My God of all comforts, I'm asking that you draw near to me now. I have suffered a loss that feels unbearable—as if part of me has been ripped away and stolen. Waves of emptiness, pain, and anxiety sweep over me at the oddest times. In those moments, I wonder how I can keep going . . . But I know that you can lift me out of the distress and fill my void with your fullness. Please show me if I need to seek additional help. If so, guide me to a good counselor. Jesus, thank you that you were willing to experience unspeakable loss for my sake. As a result, I have gained eternal life!*

# 9

## Counseling for Depression

PSYCHOEDUCATION IS VERY IMPORTANT in the treatment of every patient with depression, both by healthcare providers and counselors. Depressed people need to know what depression is and how it is treated. For example, they need to know to expect a delayed response to treatment when antidepressants and/or counseling are begun. They need to know that antidepressants are not addictive and that most side effects are mild and short-lived. They need to know that counseling is usually not a long and drawn-out process.

In psychoeducation, myths about depression and its treatment can be dispelled. For example, a moderately depressed person may want to take a leave of absence from work or study, thinking that rest from work or study may help. But in reality, inactivity and lack of engagement in the daily activities of life often make depression worse. Severely depressed people, however, are often literally unable to work or study or complete simple tasks at home. In that case, they need to be given permission to reduce professional or personal responsibilities. They needn't feel guilty about reducing responsibilities. For a season, their "work" is their recovery.

Many counselors start counseling for depression with talk therapy. Letting the counselees talk about whatever they want to talk about engages them so as to stir up their thinking, allowing the slowed-down, depressed brain to speed up and be lifted up. Depressed people usually need help reengaging life. The therapeutic relationship itself is important and has friendship vibes; the counselee has actually hired a knowledgeable friend to help process a troubled life. The relationship allows the counselee to share with someone who truly cares about the counselee and validates his/her story. Exploring a depressed person's story takes time and must be done in the context of a trusting relationship. It helps the counselee to know that the counselor has helped other people with similar, but definitely not identical, stories. Each person's story is unique. The expertise of the counselor also allows the counselee to look at his/her own life in fresh, new ways that may have helped other depressed people. Often depressed people are trapped in a depressing perspective and don't realize there are other ways to look at and address their problems.

There are many types of counseling other than psychoeducation and talk therapy that are helpful in treating depression, but our main focus will be on two types that have research-proven efficacy: cognitive-behavioral therapy (CBT) and interpersonal therapy (IPT). Of the two main counseling approaches cognitive-behavioral therapy is more of a strictly psychological approach, and interpersonal therapy is more of a psychosocial approach. Both are helpful in understanding and treating depression. As little as six weekly sessions are needed for some depressed people; twelve weeks is a common number for most. Rarely six months or more of weekly counseling is needed. I believe that understanding these two counseling approaches will take some of the mystery out of counseling, and motivate you to get the counseling help you need.

Our thoughts, behaviors, and emotions and our relationships with other people are part of the immaterial aspect of our being (see chapter 2). It should not surprise us that we can address those aspects of our being through nonbiologically based treatment, namely counseling.

## COGNITIVE-BEHAVIORAL THERAPY

Cognitive-behavioral therapy (CBT) is a psychological approach to counseling that addresses our thoughts and behaviors in order to influence our feelings. In numerous research studies, CBT has been shown to be effective in treating depression and anxiety. There is nothing mystical about this approach to counseling. In writing this section, I have been most helped by *Evidence-Based Practice of Cognitive-Behavioral Therapy* (see Selected Bibliography).

There are four principles that underlie CBT:

1. The content of our thoughts (also called our cognitions) and our thought processes are knowable. What we think and how we come

to think that way can be looked into and understood. With appropriate instruction, depressed people can become more aware of their thinking.

2. Our thoughts often mediate our emotional and behavioral responses to the various situations in which we find ourselves. The way we think about a situation often impacts how we feel or act in that situation.

3. We can intentionally modify the way we think about a situation resulting in a change in how we respond both emotionally and behaviorally. A change in how we think can help change how we feel and act.

4. We can sometimes change our thoughts and emotions just by changing our behavior.

## Common Misperceptions and Distortions

One helpful way to look at our understanding of depression is to look at common misperceptions. How we think about a situation is based (1) on the facts and circumstances of a situation and (2) on our underlying beliefs and assumptions. Our beliefs and assumptions act as filters, causing us to accurately perceive or inaccurately misperceive the implications of the facts and circumstances of a situation. A misperception of the facts and circumstances in depression is often consistent with mistaken beliefs and assumptions. In these cases, the mistaken beliefs and assumptions need to be gently challenged. I remember reading about one counselor who found four mistaken beliefs and assumptions that often predispose people to depression: (1) to be happy, I must be accepted by all people at all times; (2) if I make a mistake, that means I'm inept; (3) if someone disagrees with me, that means he does not like me; (4) my value as a person depends on what others think of me.

The chart below shows common ways depressed people misperceive things: sometimes called cognitive distortions. This chart was adapted from *Evidence-Based Practice of Cognitive-Behavioral Therapy*; the authors had adapted it from J. S. Beck:

| All-or-nothing thinking | Also called black-and-white thinking—viewing a situation as having only two possible outcomes |
| Catastrophizing | Predicting future calamity and ignoring a possible positive future |
| Fortune telling | Predicting the future with limited evidence |

| Mind reading | Believing you know what other people are thinking without them telling you what they are thinking |
|---|---|
| Disqualifying the positive | Not attending to, or giving appropriate weight to, positive information |
| Magnification/ minimization | Magnifying negative information; minimizing positive information |
| Focusing on a detail | Focusing on one negative detail rather than on the larger picture |
| Overgeneralization | Drawing exaggerated conclusions based on one occurrence or on a limited number of occurrences |
| Misattribution | Making errors in attributing the causes of various events |
| Personalization | Thinking that you caused negative things, rather than examining other possible causes |
| Emotional reasoning | Arguing that because something feels bad, it must be bad |
| Labeling | Putting a general label on someone or something, rather than describing the specific behaviors or aspects of the thing |

## Inaccurate Negative Thoughts

In addition to inaccurate beliefs and assumptions, depressed people often have inaccurate, negative thoughts that both reflect and perpetuate their depression. These inaccurate, negative thoughts often lead to inappropriate negative emotions and behaviors. These thoughts affect how depressed people feel and act. Often the inaccurate negative thoughts that accompany a situation are automatic negative thoughts (ANTs) that come to mind in any similar situation. In the book *Downcast*, Dr. Jennifer Huang Harris shares a helpful metaphor for the way thoughts affect the brain: "the repeated thoughts of depression or anxiety function like ruts in a road. Repeated thoughts wear those ruts deeper and deeper as we use these particular pathways in the brain over and over. So, it becomes easier and easier to slide down these ruts into depression, and it becomes harder and harder to get out of them and create new pathways."

To varying degrees, there may be truth in an automatic negative thought (ANT). Sometimes an ANT is completely accurate. In that case, just validating the ANT can be helpful. Sometimes there may be only a component of distorted reality in an ANT. For example, when I am disabled from depression, I think I am worthless because I cannot practice medicine.

While it is not inappropriate to gain some sense of self-worth from my profession, not all of it should come from it. Once an *inaccurate* negative thought is identified, just suppression of the thought is not likely to be effective. The depressed person must be convinced that an alternative thought is more accurate than the ANT. For example, I need to remind myself that my worth should not be wholly determined by whether I can or cannot work. In fact, in God's eyes it makes no difference.

## Evidence – Based Thinking

| Evidence for a Thought | Evidence against the Thought |
| --- | --- |
|  |  |
|  |  |
|  |  |
|  |  |

Negative Thought_____

Alternative Thought_____

An identified inaccurate negative thought needs to be challenged. To do this, the counselor and depressed person engage in some evidence-based thinking. The grid below is adapted from *Retrain Your Brain: Cognitive Behavioral Therapy in 7 Weeks*. There needs to be a collaborative effort to gather and evaluate evidence. The evidence for the negative thought and the evidence against the negative thought can be written down in separate columns. Usually, it is obvious that the negative thought is inaccurate. Then the counselee, with the counselor, needs to come up with an accurate positive alternative thought to replace the inaccurate negative one. Every time the automatic negative thought surfaces in a depressed person it needs to be challenged by the alternative positive thought.

## Evidence – Based Thinking
## Example 1

| Evidence for a Thought | Evidence against the Thought |
|---|---|
| I committed a terrible sin | I have confessed my sin and repented |
| My sin is too great to be forgiven | God is faithful and just to forgive us our sins |
| I am a shameful person | God cleanses us from all unrighteousness |
| | |

## Negative Thought: I am guilty of a sin
## Alternative Thought: I am forgiven and clean

An inaccurate negative thought may relate to our Christian faith. The negative thought in example 1 is "I am guilty of a sin." The evidence for a thought is (1) I committed a terrible sin; (2) my sin is too great to be forgiven; (3) I am a shameful person. The evidence against the thought comes from 1 John 1:9 and is (1) I have confessed my sin and repented; (2) God is faithful and just to forgive us our sin; (3) God cleanses us from all unrighteousness because Jesus dealt with all our true guilt on the cross.

Once the evidence for and against the negative thought is tallied, it should be obvious that "I am guilty of sin" is inaccurate and needs to be replaced with the believable, positive, alternative thought that "I am forgiven and clean."

Every time the ANT resurfaces, we need to substitute our believable alternative thought. At first, we may not be able to prevent the ANT from entering our minds, but we should not let it linger there. As soon as we recognize the ANT, we should immediately try to replace it with the alternative thought.

## Evidence – Based Thinking
## Example 2

| Evidence for a Thought | Evidence against the Thought |
|---|---|
| People avoid me | I don't go to church or visit friends |
| I only got a birthday card from my mother | My husband brought me flowers on my birthday |
| | No other friends know when my birthday is |
| | God loves and cares for me as His own child |

### Negative Thought: Nobody cares about me

### Alternative Thought: At least God, my husband and my mother care about me

A second example of evidence-based thinking starts with the ANT "nobody cares about me." The evidence for the thought is (1) people avoid me and (2) I got a birthday card only from my mother. The evidence against the thought is (1) I don't go to church or visit friends so I can't really say friends at church or elsewhere are avoiding me, (2) my husband brought me flowers on my birthday, (3) no friends knows when my birthday is, and (4) God loves and cares for me as his own child. The believable, realistic alternative thought is "at least God, my husband, and my mother care about me." From now on, the counselee needs to immediately substitute the ANT "nobody cares for me" with the accurate positive thought that "at least God, my husband, and my mother care about me."

Once we are convinced an alternative thought is accurate, we need to consider the consequence this alternative thought—this new way of thinking—will have on our feelings and actions. How will the alternative thought change our emotions and behaviors? Consider making a thought record, which is useful during counseling sessions and in between visits as homework.

# Breaking Negative Thought Patterns

| Situation | Thought – esp. Automatic Thoughts | Emotion | Behavior | Alternative Thought | Result - Emotion and Behavior |
|---|---|---|---|---|---|
|  |  |  |  |  |  |
|  |  |  |  |  |  |
|  |  |  |  |  |  |
|  |  |  |  |  |  |
|  |  |  |  |  |  |

The above thought record is adapted from *Evidence-Based Practice of Cognitive-Behavioral Therapy*. A thought record that helps break negative thought patterns records six things:

1. The situation that prompted the thought

2. The thought itself (especially an ANT; an automatic negative thought that we always have in similar situations)

3. The emotion (feeling) that went with the thought

4. The behavioral action previously taken in response to the thought and feeling

5. The evidence-based alternative thought

6. The result that the alternative thought will have on our emotions (feelings) and behaviors (actions)

# Breaking Negative Thought Patterns
## Example 1

| Situation | Thought – esp. Automatic Thoughts | Emotion | Behavior | Alternative Thought | Result - Emotion and Behavior |
|---|---|---|---|---|---|
| Hurtful phone call from mother | My mother's assessment of me is right | I feel worthless | I act like a doormat | I am valued by my husband | I will feel good about myself and will work on a mutually respectful relationship with my husband |

Example 1 of breaking negative thought patterns with a thought record is as follows:

1. The situation: the counselee gets a phone call from her mother who subtly puts her down once again.

2. The thought: my mother is right in her assessment of me.

3. The emotion: I feel worthless.

4. The behavior: I act like a doormat when my husband comes home from work.

5. The alternative thought: my mother is wrong in her assessment of me and I am highly valued by my husband.

6. The resulting emotion and behavior: I will feel good about myself and I will work on developing a mutually respectful relationship with my husband.

# Breaking Negative Thought Patterns
## Example 2

| Situation | Thought – esp. Automatic Thoughts | Emotion | Behavior | Alternative Thought | Result – Emotion and Behavior |
|---|---|---|---|---|---|
| Performance evaluation | I will get a negative evaluation | I feel anxious | I called in sick for work | I have been given fair evaluations in the past | I will feel competent and will improve |
|  |  |  |  |  |  |
|  |  |  |  |  |  |
|  |  |  |  |  |  |

A thought record may start with an unhelpful emotion or behavior. Then we look backward to the situation and thought, and we look forward to the alternative thought with its resulting new emotion and behavior.

Example 2 of breaking a negative thought pattern with a thought record is as follows:

1. The emotion: I feel anxious.

2. The situation: I have an upcoming performance evaluation at work.

3. The thought: I am going to get a negative performance evaluation.

4. The behavior: I called in sick for work.

5. The alternative thought: because I have been given fair evaluations in the past, I am likely to get a fair evaluation now.

6. The resulting emotion and behavior: I will feel competent, and I'm going to work on improving the areas where I am found to be deficient.

The dialogue between the counselor and counselee that resulted in the above thought record might have gone as follows:

| Counselor: | Counselee: |
| --- | --- |
| Shelly, how are you doing today? | I feel very anxious. |
| What were you doing when you felt most anxious today? | I was preparing my forms for an upcoming performance evaluation at work. |
| What were you thinking about? | I am worried that I will get a negative performance evaluation. |
| What did you do about your anxious feelings? | I called in sick for work. |
| What is the alternative thought we came up with when we did evidence-based thinking together? | Because I have been given fair evaluations in the past, I am likely to get a fair evaluation now. |
| How will your alternative thought make you feel and act differently? | I will feel competent, and I'm going to work on improving the areas where I am found to be deficient. |

## Behavioral Activation

Behavioral activation is one of the best ways to encourage change in behavior to reduce negative thoughts and emotions. Behavioral activation gets depressed people involved in dormant activities that used to give them satisfaction and/or pleasure, or activities that are necessary for everyday life. It can also be used to encourage new behaviors known to be helpful in lifting depression. Of course, depressed people need to be encouraged to embrace the discomfort and uncertainty that comes with change. Change is hard for nearly everyone but especially so for depressed people. I recently heard a quote that I agree with. "Change is difficult. Real change is real difficult."

Engaging in helpful behaviors often increases positive thinking and helpful feelings and decreases negative thinking and depressed feelings. For example, a depressed person may avoid going to social gatherings that were previously satisfying and enjoyable. This avoidance further isolates the depressed person, diminishes his/her thoughts of self-efficacy, and increases his/her feelings of inadequacy. Attending social gatherings, even if only for short periods of time, facilitates interaction with others, increases thoughts of being competent, and decreases feelings of helplessness.

People with depression need to slowly but surely become more active in spite of how they feel. However, they are often so overwhelmed that they can manage only one or two of the least difficult positive changes. Later they can address more and increasingly difficult changes.

## Behavioral Activation Hierarchy

| Activity (previously enjoyable or current necessary activity) | Degree of difficulty (1 – 10) |
|---|---|
| 1. | |
| 2. | |
| 3. | |
| 4. | |
| 5. | |
| 6. | |
| 7. | |
| 8. | |

Behavioral activation can be addressed with a hierarchy. The above grid is adapted from *Retrain Your Brain: Cognitive Behavioral Therapy in 7 Weeks*. First, the depressed person lists a number of activities he/she formerly engaged in but now avoids including necessary activities. Then on a scale of one to ten, the person rates how hard it will be to reengage in each activity. The depressed person starts by reengaging the least difficult activity and then works through the hierarchy. Success with less difficult things encourages commitment to address more difficult things and success breeds success. Another behavioral activation hierarchy can be used to introduce helpful new behaviors.

## Behavioral Activation Hierarchy

| Activity (previously enjoyable or current necessary activity)10 | Degree of difficulty (1 – 10) |
|---|---|
| 1. Exercise | 4 |
| 2. Make dinner | 3 |
| 3. Go to a movie | 2 |
| 4. Attend church | 6 |
| 5. Call a good friend | 3 |
| 6. Visit a good friend | 5 |
| 7. Pay bills | 4 |
| 8. Go to work | 10 |

In the above example of a behavioral activation hierarchy, the counselee lists (1) exercise, (2) make dinner, (3) go to a movie, (4) attend church, (5) call a good friend, (6) visit a good friend, (7) pay bills, and (8) go to work. The first behavior the counselee needs to commit to is "go to a movie" rated two (item 3) and the last is "go to work" rated ten (item 8). By reengaging in previously pleasurable or currently necessary or helpful activities, his/her mood usually improves, and he/she becomes more confident and has a greater sense of self-efficacy.

Behavioral activation can be helpful in the specific area of one's spiritual life. When anxious depressed Christians have allowed a season of worry and pressures to push God out of their lives, they might, step by step, reintroduce God back into their lives through worship, Bible study, meditation, prayer, reading good books by Christian authors, listening to faithful music, and fostering friendships with other believers in church, in smaller groups and one on one. Remember, this is all often extremely hard for anxious depressed Christians to do, but every little movement back toward God is a step in the right direction. God eagerly awaits his children's return. The prophet Jeremiah promises, "You will seek me [the Lord] and find me, when you seek me with all your heart. I will be found by you" (Jeremiah 29:13–14).

## INTERPERSONAL PSYCHOTHERAPY

Interpersonal psychotherapy (IPT), like CBT, has been shown in numerous research studies to be effective in treating many who suffer from depression. There is nothing mystical about interpersonal therapy. IPT's approach to counseling, however, is much different from the CBT approach. As the name suggests, IPT focuses on relationships. We have seen how we are social beings (chapter 2), so it should not surprise us that counseling in regard to relationships would help those with depression. Interpersonal problems can cause depression or be the result of depression or both. In general, IPT focuses on current relational problems, rather than past problems such as childhood relational trauma. Remote relationships are usually addressed only when they significantly relate to current interpersonal conflict. Even then, IPT usually addresses those remote relationships only briefly.

Focusing on relationships in two broad categories is especially helpful in treating depression: role disputes and role transitions. A substantial amount of this section is adapted from *The Guide to Interpersonal Psychotherapy* (see Selective Bibliography).

## Role Disputes

Role disputes involve two people in a relationship where their different needs and expectations are causing conflict. When looking at role disputes (e.g., marital conflict or job dissatisfaction), the counselor examines with the counselee current problematic relationships and collaboratively discovers ways to positively impact them. Sometimes the counselee needs help to even identify his/her needs. Once a need is identified, the counselee should work, with help, toward learning how to express his/her need in a constructive way. The counselor can also help identify differing expectations that should change for a healthy relationship. Where each person stubbornly persists in thinking his/her expectation is the best one, the counselor may work toward an acceptable compromise. (By the way, most of us are stubborn in our own ideas when there is conflict.) In an example of a role dispute, one marriage partner may feel left out of the activities his/her spouse is involved in. The counselor might help find ways that the needs of the "neglected" spouse can be met by joining in at least some of the partner's activities. If there is no good way to do this, the counselor might help the couple identify new activities that they can enjoy together. If role disputes are not satisfactorily addressed, it can lead to bitterness and resentment that fuels the fire of depression.

## Role Transitions

Role transitions are significant changes in relationships that cause distress, often relating to a person's life cycle, for example, leaving home for college or retiring from employment. A life cycle change can churn up stress in anyone—more so with those who suffer from depression. A competent counselor helps counselees identify difficult transitions and collaboratively discover positive ways to adjust to the changes. The counselor may help counselees cope with change or, even better, empower them to initiate change. A negative view of a change can sometimes be turned into a positive view. You may imagine together how a change could improve one's response to a troubling situation. Although adjustment to new situations is required in role transitions, one of the hardest parts of the transition is the loss of or change in one or more relationships. As we have said before depressed people often find change extremely difficult.

While CBT focuses more on problematic thoughts (cognitions) and behaviors that result in problematic feelings, IPT has a stronger emphasis on the feelings (emotions) themselves, especially as they relate to other people.

We used many insights from IPT when earlier we addressed common distressing feelings associated with depression in chapter 8. Feelings related to role disputes and role transitions are often uncomfortable and threatening. In IPT, depressed people are encouraged to express their feelings in the safe environment of a counselor's office. Merely expressing strong emotions can decrease the negative power the emotions have over the counselee. The counselor also normalizes the counselee's feelings by helping him/her see that (1) most people would have similar feelings in a similar conflicted relationship, and (2) the feelings, at least in part, are often appropriate reactions to distressing interpersonal relationships.

Depressed people often perceive uncomfortable, threatening feelings, such as anger directed toward others, as "bad" and then jump to the conclusion that they are bad people. But examining such feelings is helpful in identifying the source of interpersonal conflict. Discovering the meaning of strong feelings is also helpful in resolving the conflict. For example, anger is often a sign that you have been hurt by another person. The hurt needs to be addressed to resolve the anger. When a depressed person's anger is expressed in an uncontrolled fashion, it can add to a burden of guilt. Uncontrolled anger can also create even more conflict in an already problematic relationship. To successfully address the anger, the guilt as well as the hurt need to be addressed. One counseling tool useful for the counselor to help the depressed person who struggles with anger is anger management.

On the one hand, interpersonal problems can lead to depression. On the other hand, depression can lead to interpersonal problems. In either case, the interpersonal conflict needs to be addressed. Otherwise, the stress of the conflict will continue unabated or even escalate, aggravating the depression.

An early task in IPT is identifying the connection between the onset of the symptoms of depression and the onset or worsening of stressful relationships. This helps the counselee to recognize that the conflictual relationships need to be addressed to resolve the depression. Recognizing the conflict may motivate the counselee to address the relational problems he/she has been trying to avoid.

The counselor helps identify beneficial versus maladaptive communication patterns—verbal and nonverbal patterns in a stressful relationship. The counselor then helps the depressed person resolve the problematic communication patterns. As the communication in stressful relationships improves, the symptoms of depression often improve as well.

Sometimes depressed people resist working on problematic relationships because they think they have already tried everything. Usually the counselor can help these pessimists identify a new or modified approach and provide the tools they need to bring about a desirable change. For example, depressed people are often averse to confronting people who have hurt or threatened them. The counselor may need to help depressed people be less passive using a tool called assertiveness training. Often new communication patterns such as assertiveness need to be practiced with the counselor. Role-playing may feel childish at first but is often incredibly useful in situations that would benefit from assertiveness. The emotions generated by a confrontation may be so overwhelming that the depressed person will be unable to communicate in a healthy way unless he/she has practiced ahead of time. If an approach to resolving a stressful relationship doesn't work, it need not be viewed as a failure. Rather, it can be viewed as a learning experience that uncovers helpful information that will be used to develop another modified or new approach.

IPT counselors can be especially helpful with complicated grief. Grief always involves a role transition. When a loved one dies, a very important relationship is severed. The loss forces a role transition. Because of the needs of a dying person, the caretaker may not have maintained and nurtured other important relationships. In this case, the death creates an interpersonal void. To fill this void, past relationships may need to be renewed and new relationships formed. Sometimes the grieving person may have a sort of role dispute with the deceased. The counselee may feel angry at and/or abandoned by the deceased. These feelings need to be expressed and worked through, as well as the underlying hurt.

Although CBT usually addresses the least difficult problems first to enable the depressed person to experience an initial successful change, IPT often addresses the most difficult problems early on. To the counselees, the IPT approach is reassuring in that their biggest problems are taken seriously.

An IPT counselor generally tries to help counselees deal with one problematic relationship at a time. As depressed people gain success in communication in one problematic relationship, they are more likely try out their new knowledge and skills in different relationships. What is learned from resolving one conflictual relationship can be helpful in resolving others.

## DIGGING DEEPER

Sometimes current relational problems cannot be adequately addressed without examining, in detail, childhood relationships. A child's unmet needs like lack of affirmation or emotional neglect, can lead to profound feelings of distress. The distress is even more profound when there has been physical, sexual, verbal, or emotional abuse. The child develops ways to cope with the distress in order to decrease anxiety, feel more secure, and maintain a semblance of self-esteem. These patterns of interacting with others in a difficult family environment may be internalized and negatively influence later relationships. A child also intuitively understands the rules of his/her family and often takes on a role that meets the needs of the dysfunctional family more than his/her own needs. Finally, a child incorporates some of the traits of his/her parents and discards others. In the process, the child may incorporate some bad traits and discard some good ones.

Often deeply rooted problems that are traced back to childhood require in-depth, prolonged counseling. One benefit of this intense counseling is that the therapeutic relationship between the counselor and counselee becomes, in and of itself, healing. This may be the first healthy relationship the depressed person has ever experienced. The way the person learns to interact verbally and emotionally with the counselor can lead to healthier relationships with others. Other relationship-focused therapies, such as IPT, have more research backing for their effectiveness in treating depression than does this kind of in-depth counseling. That may be because it is very hard to do research on this type of counseling. Each therapeutic relationship is so unique that it is hard to fit them into the well-defined categories needed for research. Unfortunately, the time commitment and cost of this type of counseling limits its usefulness for many depressed people.

## CHOOSING A COUNSELOR

As with choosing a healthcare provider, you need to trust and have confidence in your counselor especially if you are clinically depressed. Anyone can call themselves a counselor, so first check on his/her credentials, which usually includes two to five years of postgraduate training and licensing by the state they practice in. Call and find out what the degree of your prospective counselor is and if you are not sure what the degree means, Google it. Your healthcare provider may also have a recommendation.

Two traits that are particularly important in a counselor are empathy and authenticity. Research studies have shown that the right fit with your counselor improves the likelihood you will be helped by the counseling. If you do not trust and have confidence in your counselor after four sessions (at the latest), you need to find another one. One caveat is that you as the counselee must be authentic and honest with your counselor. Effective counseling requires honest self-examination and sharing what you have discovered about yourself, and that can be frightening.

The approach used by a counselor may be important to you. If you think you would prefer CBT over IPT or vice versa, you can ask before you make an appointment what approach he/she uses most. Some counselors use only one or the other. Others use multiple approaches. Using multiple approaches is not automatically better. Some counselors who use different approaches may use only one approach with a particular patient. If one approach has not begun to help you by the end of twelve sessions (at the latest), a different approach should be tried or a different counselor, or both.

There is considerable controversy among Christians as to whether the counselor should be a Christian. Because counseling often deals with value-laden issues, it is certainly helpful to have someone who shares your Christian values. That being said, I would rather have a competent non-Christian counselor than an incompetent Christian one for clinical depression. Just because someone thinks they are competent to counsel a moderately or more seriously depressed person does not necessarily mean they are competent. Fortunately, most Christian counselees have enough values in common with non-Christian counselors that they can still be very helpful.

Two relevant examples of values that most Christians and non-Christians share are the importance (1) of stable, loving relationships and (2) of replacing untrue, automatic negative thoughts with true positive thoughts. By common grace, many secular counseling approaches are consistent with Christian beliefs. Also, most good counselors will try to respect your religious values even if they do not share them. Unfortunately, they don't always succeed. If you sense that there may be a conflict of values, you should get input from your pastor or priest. In fact, you should consider meeting with your pastor or priest on a regular basis for spiritual guidance during your depression. Though your depression is not likely to be primarily due to spiritual problems, depression often brings with it a chance to make progress in your spiritual as well as mental health. In all events, if your counselor is hostile to your faith or thinks it irrelevant, you need to find another counselor.

Some pastors and priest are well trained in dealing with depression. If you trust and have confidence in your pastor and if you are being helped, you may not need the help of another counselor. A trained pastor or priest will know when to refer you to a healthcare provider or a professional counselor. If you sense that you are not getting the help you need from your pastor or priest, you don't need to get that cleric's permission to seek additional help.

# 10

## Friends and Family Can Help

### MY GRATITUDE

BEFORE MY LAST DEPRESSION, I did not spend much time with friends. Now I meet with a group of three other fellow believers every week to study the Bible and especially for fellowship. Once a week, I have breakfast with a physician colleague. About once a month, I meet for coffee with an Anglican priest. I have two friends with whom I talk on the phone with every two weeks. One is a retired pastor I have known for decades. One is a man who befriended me during my last depression. There are a number of other men suffering from depression, or other mental stresses or illnesses, with whom I keep in regular contact. I also look forward every month to our depression support group. All these relationships are precious to me. I did not have such close friendships before my last depression. The friendships that I did have, I did not adequately nurture or allow myself to be nurtured by them.

Depressed Christians may need to be reminded that God sees us just as we are and still deeply loves us. We need to enjoy God's acceptance of us so as to allow other people's disapproval of us to matter less. It is helpful, of course, if the people around us love us and accept us even when they have seen us at our weakest and worst. This acceptance is the way family, friends, and the church can really help. These helpers do not have to believe many of the negative things we depressed people say about ourselves, but they should reassure us that they would love us no less if those things were really true.

I think of my wife, Fenni. Fenni had known and loved me for only a few months when I suffered my medical school depression. She had the perfect opportunity to bail, but she didn't. Throughout our lives together, Fenni has been my earthly loving and loyal rock. (God is my heavenly loving and loyal rock.) Never once did Fenni's frustration show. In fact, she'll tell you she never was frustrated or upset by my depression (this is not common in those who care for depressed people). Surely Fenni must have been specially gifted by the Holy Spirit to care for me.

## COMPASSION AND COMFORT

The caring and faithful presence of a person who is not demanding or judgmental is often really helpful to a depressed person. Being that person is a very demanding but potentially satisfying role. The good Samaritan acted compassionately toward the robbed and beaten man on the deserted road; while others walked by, he was compassionate and it was at his own expense in terms of mental energy, time, and money.

If you know someone who is broken by depression, consider coming alongside that person as an affirming, nonjudgmental presence. Depressed people need to feel that it is safe to be weak around a person who comes alongside them. They need someone they trust to share the burden of their brokenness. It usually takes time for depressed people to be open with you about their weaknesses and sin. You need to earn their trust, because they rightly recognize that you may hurt them. But having someone who comes beside you, who tunes into your inner world and reflects with you on your painful story, is powerfully healing medicine. In 2 Corinthians 7:5–6, Paul commends his coworker Titus for coming to his side when he was suffering. "For even when we came into Macedonia, our bodies had no rest, but we were afflicted at every turn—fighting without and fear within. But God, who comforts the downcast, comforted us by the coming of Titus." The most prolific New Testament author, Paul, was afflicted, fearful, and downcast, but a friend came to him and comforted him. In so much that is written about depression, there is little about how important comfort alone can be when we are suffering. If all we bring to a depressed person is a little comfort, we have served a worthwhile role.

## ASSURING AND LISTENING

If you think a friend or family member may be depressed, talk to him/her about it. Don't be concerned that he/she will feel insulted or angry. A truly depressed person will likely be grateful that you opened the conversation on this painful topic. Even if they turn out not to be depressed, most people will appreciate your concern.

Here are some things you can say early on in your conversations with a depressed person:

1. You are not alone. I intend to be there for you no matter what.

2. I may not be able to fully understand how you feel, but I want to try to understand.

3. I love you and care about you and want to help in any way I can.

4. Please tell me what I can do to help. Would going to a movie help? Would praying with you help? Would you just like me to hang out with you? Or do you need to be alone now?

5. You are important to me. I can't imagine life without you.

6. Try to hold on to one more day. If not one more day, one more hour. If not one more hour, one more minute. If you can't hold on anymore, we need to get help right away.

Your main role in a relationship with a depressed person is to be a loving, empathetic listener. Research has shown that brain activity of a depressed person actually changes in response to caring relationships. Listening is more important than giving advice. You should not try to "fix" the problem. Rather, try to get the depressed person to talk about thoughts and feelings and try to understand them. Be prepared to listen to the same thing over and over, as depressed people often ruminate. They can't help it, so don't chastise them. If you can't helpfully listen after a period of time, take a break. Tell the depressed person that you will talk with him/her again at some time you set for later. Having patience is hard, but recovery from depression is a slow process. Often it feels like your friend or family member is taking two steps forward and one step back, or worse—one step forward and two steps back.

If the depressed person hurts you or lets you down by words or actions, don't ignore it but don't overreact either. Try not to take it personally, but if you do, gently and lovingly address the problem. If you don't address it, you may become resentful and unintentionally hurt the depressed person because of your bitterness. Remember that, like anyone, depressed people are likely to repeat the same negative behaviors. Peter once said, "'Lord, how often will my brother sin against me, and I forgive him? As many as seven times?' Jesus said to him, 'I do not say to you seven times, but seventy times seven'" (Matthew 18:21–22).

Depression saps motivation and energy. You may need to schedule appointments with the depressed person's healthcare provider, counselor, or clergy. You may even need to take this person to appointments. These healers may want to hear about your concerns. Consider helping with domestic responsibilities such as house cleaning or fixing a meal or shopping. But don't let yourself get burned out. Encourage your depressed friend or family member to join you in something enjoyable—maybe a walk. Don't readily accept no for an answer unless he/she refuses in spite of your persistence. Having said that, try to be sensitive to times when the depressed person really does need to be alone.

## BE AWARE OF YOUR OWN SELF NEEDS

If you know someone with depression, you can be a part of his/her healing. But you must take care of yourself. It is not a selfish act. You need to be strong enough emotionally to help your friend or family member. Depressed people can unintentionally be very demanding. Most family and friends of depressed people cannot weather the stress without some unwanted thoughts and feelings. It is easy for you yourself to become depressed, anxious, frustrated, angry, guilt ridden, exhausted, rejected, unappreciated, unloved, inadequate, and/or helpless. Frustration and helplessness are particularly common feelings. These are normal reactions, but you should talk about these feelings with a trusted friend or clergyperson. You are not betraying the depressed person's trust by talking with others about the stress you are experiencing and how it makes you feel. You are being strengthened for service. You may even want to become a part of or start a caregiver support group. If your feelings are overwhelming, consider getting some counseling for yourself.

Do not give up things that are important to you. It is important that you set clear boundaries in terms of time and mental energy. You can only do so much. Collaboratively discuss with the depressed person the expectations that you each should have. Remember that you are not the healthcare provider, counselor, or clergy. They can provide help that you can't or shouldn't offer. Your role is as a good friend or family member who really cares and wants to help, but not in an overbearing fashion.

You might want to recommend a depression support group. If you cannot find one, consider finding one online or starting one yourself. Some churches, hospitals, and behavioral health centers sponsor grief recovery groups and depression support groups. The only absolutes of leading a depression support group are having a facilitator to keep everyone on track, strict confidentiality, and a recognition that what works for one person will not always work for another. Often, however, what works for one person gives insight to another person. And just being able to tell your story to empathetic listeners in your support group is often helpful in depression.

*Downcast* recommends four important things to remember if you are a caregiver for a depressed person:

1. You're not responsible for how they feel

2. You're not responsible for curing their depression

3. Try to distinguish between the person and their depression

4. Being depressed does not take away a person's responsibility for their actions and words or entitle them to bad behavior

Hearing a story about how depression affects a family and how the family can impact a depressed person may be helpful. Kathryn Greene-McCreight's extended story of bipolar depression in *Darkness Is My Only Companion* is helpful to me:

> This leads me to a warning about children of people who live with mental illnesses. Most children are very sensitive and perceptive; they understand much more than we give them credit for. Parents should explain to their children what the nature of the problem is, or the children may create scenarios in their minds that are worse than the realities of the situation. They may even blame themselves. Our children pretended they were comfortable with Mommy's spiritual, psychological, and physical absences behind the door of the bedroom, but they became absolutely unhinged when I went into the hospital. Grades slipped; moods dropped. Our son became more aggressive, and our daughter withdrew. My husband and I were so embarrassed at the hospitalization that we did not even tell teachers at the children's school. This was a big mistake that at the time we did not recognize.
>
> We had not prepared the children well enough for my first hospital stay and did not share the details with them. Children need communication at times even as horrible as these, but it must be judicious communication. Do not mention suicidal

thoughts or gestures. Just something simple. "Mommy is sick. She is very sad. She needs to go to the hospital. She will get better and be home soon. The doctors will take good care of her." Even telling children that "Mommy has a brain disorder" is better than saying nothing, or than saying her heart hurts. Children have heard about heart attacks and know how serious they are. Don't bring in half-truths for the sake of protecting children. Speak matter-of-factly, quietly, calmly. Stress that the hospital is a good place for those who are sick. Tell them that it is no one's fault and that the doctors are doing their job . . .

So family is very important. The support of a loving spouse is very comforting. My husband, Matthew, is the most loving and most patient partner I could ever imagine. I could never have asked for more. I would question how he was putting up with this blob of a wife, or with the zippy version, with no in-betweens. The chores of the household fell on him: laundry, cooking, shopping, child minding. And he still had a full-time job, which he had to cut back. He is a helpmate given by the grace of God. I shudder to think what I would have done without his support and encouragement. Maybe my suicidal urges would have become reality: in many ways I owe my life to my husband.

My mother came to stay with the children and to help run the household while I was in the hospital. I don't remember how long she was with us, but it was not a short stint. She bore the yeoman's burden while I was in the hospital, trying to relieve my husband of cooking and cleaning and ferrying the children to and from school. This allowed Matthew to return to work and kept the children on a fairly even keel. I don't even remember any more than this, because the time is still fuzzy in my memory, and according to my psychiatrist, it always will be. Some things I remember quite clearly, and others I can't recall at all. That is probably a mercy.

Of course, there are many ways family and friends can hinder the healing process of depressed people. You may not understand depression and not get the help you need to understand it, so you can be a more empathetic listener and supportive friend. You may accept that the person is depressed but not encourage and assist getting help though medicine and/or counseling. You may not validate the distressing feelings depressed people often have and so seem to ignore their pain. You may not gently challenge untrue or only partially true thoughts that may be contributing to depression. You may not encourage healing behaviors—of course this must be done without making those who are depressed feel guilty if they just can't do them. It is important to empathize with the way other people and events have contributed to a person's depression. But sometimes a depressed person may settle into an unhelpful long-term victim role and thereby avoid taking any significant responsibility for their healing from their depression. If you are discouraged or frustrated that you are not helping a depressed person, consider getting counseling for yourself to gain more insight into depression and its treatment. Counseling can also give you much needed encouragement for all that you are doing in trying to help.

The book *Downcast* has an especially good chapter on "The Crucial Role of Family, Friends and the Church" (see Selective Bibliography).

# 11

## Four Spiritual Myths about Depression

LET'S LOOK AT FOUR spiritual myths about suffering held by some Christians. These myths are especially relevant to suffering caused by depression. Dr. Gordon Hugenberger, my friend, teacher, and former pastor, was especially helpful in writing about some of these spiritual myths and the subsequent spiritual helps.

1. Depression is usually the result of a specific sin or a sinful lifestyle.

2. Depression is due to a lack of faith.

3. Happiness is a choice.

4. Suffering always comes directly from Satan.

### DEPRESSION AND SIN

The first spiritual myth about depression is that it is usually the result of a specific sin or a sinful lifestyle.

You may think that sin is the main reason for your depression. You may even have heard that *sin* led you into depression. This is not likely, so don't believe yourself or others who say so. I'm not saying that you are sinless. You are a sinner saved by grace; like me, you sin regularly. But sin is rarely the main factor leading to depression. If it were, getting over depression would be much easier.

All sin must, of course, be dealt with. Because Christ died for your sin, you can confess your sin, repent (turn around and change directions), and, when possible, make amends. Then in the eyes of God, you are completely cleansed from your sin. You are no longer guilty. If sin were the main cause of your depression, you should promptly begin getting better. But if you are a clinically depressed, committed Christian, there is a good chance that you have already confessed and repented of your sin—and not just once but many times. You are likely to be still depressed and dragged down by shame and inappropriate guilt.

## Looking at Sin

Part of the problem in talking about sin in modern Western culture is that the word *sin* sometimes means something different in modern times than in the biblical world. In modern Western culture, the word *sin* is not thought of as having the many different meanings it has in the Bible. This can be confusing.

In the Old Testament, six different Hebrew word roots are translated as "sin," "sinful," "sinner," etc. The three most common Hebrew words for *sin* in the Old Testament mean (1) "to be found mistaken, to be found deficient or lacking, to be at fault, to miss a specified goal or mark"; (2) "willful, knowledgeable violation of a godly norm or standard"; and (3) "real moral guilt or iniquity before God."

In the New Testament, *sin* most often refers to "individual wrong thoughts or actions." The word *sinner* in the New Testament often refers to a person alienated from God, especially "a life which is not oriented around obedience to the will of God" (citing "sin" in the *Anchor Bible Dictionary*).

If defined as being found deficient or lacking or missing a specified goal or mark, sin is a significant factor in most depression. Nearly all depressed people would acknowledge that this aspect of sin is a component of their depression. Nearly all depressed people wish their lives were different; they wish for fuller lives that are not deficient or lacking, lives that reach goals of renewed joy, motivation, energy, godly self-worth, and the like. In my opinion, counselors who fixate on sin have missed the mark themselves. They are addressing the wrong problems. Because they are sinner in this sense they have been hurtful rather than helpful.

But the common understanding of the word *sin* by most modern Westerners, Christian and non-Christian alike, is that of willful, knowledgeable violation of a recognized norm or standard. It is confusing to most depressed people to use the word *sin*, because it implies to them that they have entertained thoughts, spoken words, or done acts of willful knowledge-able disobedience that have led to the depression. Adding to the confusion is that in modern Western society, previously shared and well-recognized norms and standards have eroded, and current social norms and standards are shifting. The Christian faith has much to say about godly norms and standards, and discussing them as they relate to the depression is an important aspect of Christian counseling.

Often non-Christians and Christians alike don't realize that some of their goals might not be what God deems best for them—getting into the best university, seeking a different job just for the pay increase or to climb the corporate ladder, focusing on a flawless face or body, and so forth.

*Sin,* as used in the modern sense (i.e., willful, knowledgeable violation of a recognized norm or standard), is usually not the main factor in depression. If present, it is usually one of many causes, contributors to, and/or triggers of depression. If present, this kind of sin is often only a minor factor in the depression. That is not to say that any sin is insignificant, only that it is often a minor factor in terms of its likelihood of causing, contributing to, and/or triggering depression. On the other hand, there are often those who consider themselves spiritually healthy with minimal sin in their lives. They often fail to recognize that sins of omission (things left undone) are just as serious as sins of commission (things done). Not doing what is right, good, and just is just as serious as doing what is wrong, evil, and unjust.

Not infrequently, an excessively sensitive conscience in a depressed Christian will be completely demoralized by a sin that healthy minds can promptly attend to with confession and repentance. Worse, of course, is that some "healthy minds" will ignore their sin.

Sometimes certain types of sin, in the modern sense, are significant causal factors in depression, especially sins that bring disgrace or result in major unwelcome changes in life. Discovered sexual sins are likely to trigger depression. If a man is caught in adultery, which destroys his marriage and devastates his family, he may become depressed. Any Christian adulterer should be depressed (not necessarily clinically depressed), at least for a while. Too often, however, he walks away from the marriage unscathed, but triggering depression in his wife and children. The depressed wife and children are the victims of another person's sin, not their own.

## Looking at a Sinful Lifestyle

In most minds, *sinful lifestyle* refers to a select number of generally unacceptable activities such as prostitution, drug dealing, or abuse of elderly people through scams. Most non-Christians and Christians understand "sinful lifestyle" as a life that repeatedly, consciously rebels against well-recognized norms or standards. Sinful lifestyle in this sense is usually not helpful in discussing the many lifestyles that can cause, contribute to, or trigger depression, because these sinful lifestyles are so uncommon in depressed people.

But a *sinful lifestyle* that is defined as "a life not oriented around obedience to the will of God" can become a significant factor in depression. The phrase is not often used of a Christian who focuses too much on the accumulation of wealth. The rich person may experience a midlife crisis, questioning the meaning of life, when he/she discovers wealth has not brought life meaning. Or, in a perfectionistic lifestyle, perfectionists demand more of themselves than God requires or desires. However, the perfectionists may never have considered that their perfectionism is contrary to God's will. They are not consciously rebelling against well-recognized godly norms or standards—often they don't even know what the godly norms or standards should be. The negative effects of perfectionism are rarely mentioned in sermons or Sunday school. Godly counseling can help set new goals and expectations that help perfectionists be released from depression's tight grip.

If counselors insist on using the phrase *sinful lifestyle* in the context of counseling depressed people, they should ensure that the person understands that all Christian have sinful lifestyles, including those who are gossips, are easily angered, are often envious, find it hard to forgive, etc. All of us have "sinful lifestyles" in this sense. Yet not all of us become depressed as a result of these lifestyles. Those who are already vulnerable to depression are usually the ones who become depressed.

## Our Fallen Nature

Always one component of depression is our fallen human nature. Adam and Eve's sin resulted in human weaknesses as well as a sinful nature. Two of many human weaknesses are pain and death. In the garden of Eden after the first couple's rebellion, God said to Eve, "in pain you shall bring forth children" (Genesis 3:16). Depression is one of many painful human weaknesses—an especially painful one. Depression is not a sin; it is a mental weakness and not a character flaw. To Adam, who also rebelled, God said, "to dust you shall return" in death (v. 19). Grief is, of course, caused by the human weakness of mortality, which Adam's sin resulted in. No one would consider grief, a self-limited form of depression, to be the result of sin in the modern sense of the word. Sometimes human weakness and sin coexist in depression. For example, an alcoholic, who has a biological addictive tendency, may seriously injure another person in a drunk-driving accident. This may trigger a depression. In this situation, confession of sin, repentance, and making amends are necessary, in addition to addressing the addiction and the depression. Jesus often forgave sin at the same time that he healed sickness.

## DEPRESSION AND FAITH

The second spiritual myth is that depression is due to a lack of faith. Again, in my experience, depression is not often due to a lack of faith, though the depressed person may think that it is. The famous nineteenth-century preacher Charles Spurgeon, whom we met earlier, at times thought his depression was due to a lack of faith. If Spurgeon was right about his own lack of faith, then all Christians, not only those who are depressed, have a lack of faith. Of course, in one sense, none of us has sufficient faith.

Fortunately, Jesus requires from us only "faith like a grain of mustard seed" (one of the smallest seeds in Palestine) to move mountains (Matthew 17:20). Of course, Jesus does not want our faith to remain a seed, and he often uses suffering to grow us into a large mustard bush (the size of a small tree) of faith.

Depressed Christians may actually spend more time trying to bolster their faith than those who consider themselves spiritually healthy. Depressed Christians often recognize their desperate dependence on God more than those who are not depressed. Of course, all Christians should remember the remarkable faith of the heroes of the faith, such as Job and the prophet Jeremiah, whose testimonies of their depressions we considered earlier. One common struggle Christians experience in depression is how God can be so good and loving and allow them to experiences such pain. Most depressed Christians struggle with "theodicy"—how can God permit suffering.

Suggesting that depressed Christians are less spiritual than others adds to the guilt that they already inappropriately experience from their mental illness. It is cruel to project more false guilt onto them. A friend of mine who struggled with anxiety, fear, and dread wrote, "Serving up a load of guilt with a side dish of failure to someone already burdened with pain and discouragement is not helpful. It can even spark resentment . . . turned upward toward God . . . turned outward toward the person giving the advice . . . or turned inward toward oneself." I have experienced this resentment and have had to repent of it. Those of us who care about a depressed person don't want to trigger this kind of resentment. We may even need to repent and make amends for things we have said in the past. If you are in this position,

I suggest you go to the one you have said something potentially hurtful to and confess your sin. It will take a heavy burden off that person's shoulders. It will show that you really care.

When we are depressed, we should, of course, try to bolster our faith even more. Daily spiritual disciplines such as Bible reading (especially the Psalms), prayer, and listening to Christian songs may bring comfort, but these disciplines alone, in and of themselves, don't usually heal depression. Severely depressed people often don't have the concentration needed to read the Bible or pray for any significant length of time. Maybe, however, they can read one relevant verse (some of these verses are in Appendix C) or say a brief prayer like "help me, Jesus" (see Appendix D for helpful prayers from someone who has suffered like you).

Sometimes a depressed person gets partial relief from depression at worship services, especially through favorite spiritual songs and hymns and liturgical rites, including celebrating communion. Being a guest at the Lord's Supper every week has been especially helpful to me when I am depressed. I am reminded of how much Jesus loves me and how his death and resurrection has redeemed and recreated me. Often the sermons, even good ones, are too demanding intellectually for me to concentrate on.

Churches should be places where depressed people can find *love* and *encouragement*. If you are depressed and don't find your current church to be loving and encouraging, try to talk with one of the pastors or priests. Pessimism may be like a blinder that prevents you from seeing the love and encouragement that is indeed present in the congregation. If there are significant problems in the church that do not change, you may need to find another church. This, of course, takes initiative that may be difficult for a depressed person to muster.

Sometimes depressed believers need to lean on the faith of other Christians. The Gospel of Mark tells the story of a man with paralysis whose four friends removed part of a roof and lowered him into the crowded house where Jesus was teaching. Jesus saw "their faith"—the faith of the friends, not only of the paralytic. He then forgave the sins of the paralytic and healed him (Mark 2:1–12). Jesus' priority was to forgive sin and then to heal. His supernatural healing was in part so that people would recognize him as the Son of God who had the authority to forgive sins. Many, many times when I have been depressed, I have had to lean on the faith of my wife, children, and friends. I believe God often looked at my faith through eyes of the faith of others who cared for me.

## DEPRESSION AND CHOICE

The third spiritual myth is that happiness is a choice. What a ridiculous, insensitive thing to tell a depressed person! Who would choose unhappiness? The depressed person cannot simply choose to feel happy. Choice is a brain activity of the will, and the will of a depressed person is broken. The nineteenth-century Anglican author of *Jane Eyre*, Charlotte Bronte, who had experienced depression, once wrote, "No mockery in this world ever sounds to me so hollow as that of being told to cultivate happiness."

Although we cannot experience instantaneous happiness by choice, we do need to slowly but surely replace negative, false, unbiblical thoughts with positive, true, biblical thoughts. Cognitive-behavioral therapy, which was addressed earlier, has shown us how important it is to challenge our automatic negative thoughts if our negative feelings are going to slowly change over time. In this very limited sense, happiness is a choice, but it usually occurs with very small improvements over very long periods of time. We also need to try to make small helpful changes in our behaviors.

The psalmist sings in Psalm 100:2, "Serve the Lord with gladness!" Paul says in Philippians 4:4, "Rejoice in the Lord always; again, I will say, rejoice." These verses are not commands that can be disobeyed. They are words of encouragement that don't always bring gladness to depressed people. Christians are not immune to sadness, but they should sometimes try to find some joy in the midst of prolonged sadness. Depressed Christians should sometimes put themselves in situations where they may be able to rejoice in the Lord, possibly during songs or hymns at church. There may be times it will bring a small measure of joy for a short period of time. But this joy is unlikely to surface even briefly when people are in the deep despair of severe depression. Even those who are less depressed will not *always* feel joyful. I am thankful for Psalm 88, which we discussed earlier. If depressed people have tried to rejoice and yet feel no joy, they should not add on an additional burden of inappropriate guilt. They have done what the Bible exhorted them to do; they have tried to rejoice. I am so thankful that God expects no more from me than trying.

The teaching of rejoicing always should be balanced with the Bible's recognition that there is "a time to weep, and a time to laugh" (Ecclesiastes 3:4). Many Christians who are laughing now should weep. If they have a hard time weeping, maybe they should ask for tears. They may not have realized how perilously close they came to damaging their soul with something they thought, said, or did. They may have injured a depressed person by pushing that person to rejoice when they couldn't.

To take Scriptures such as "rejoice in the Lord always" out of the context of the whole Bible is a grave error. It ignores a whole genre of biblical literature, including the psalms of lament. As I write this, I have a niece who is pregnant with a female fetus that will die from a serious heart defect within hours or days of her birth. Her doctors had recommended an abortion, but thankfully she does not consider that an option for her. I wouldn't dare tell her to rejoice in the Lord always. Her father, my brother Wesley, says they are being taught how to lament in the Lord.

## DEPRESSION AND SATAN

The fourth spiritual myth is that suffering always comes directly from Satan, his demons, and evil or unclean spirits. The three places in the Bible where I find Satan clearly causing physical or mental suffering, other than demon possession, are in Job 2:3–8; Luke 13:10–17, and 2 Corinthians 12:7.

After killing Job's children and destroying his belongings (Job 1:8–22), "[Satan] struck Job with loathsome sores from the sole of his foot to the crown of his head" (Job 2:7). This painful, degrading skin disease along with the previous tragedies contributed to Job's severe depression. Interestingly, Job never knew that Satan was at work behind the scenes. It was not something he needed to know to be healed. We also know that God set the limit for Satan's attack on Job (Job 1:12; 2:6). So even if Satan is attacking you in your depression, he is not doing more than God, your good and loving Father, permits.

Luke reports on the healing of a woman with "a disabling spirit for eighteen years" (Luke 13:11). Jesus recognized that "Satan bound [her] for eighteen years" (v. 16). Remarkably, when Jesus laid his hands on her he merely said, "Woman, you are freed from your disability" (v. 12). He did not verbally cast out an evil or unclean spirit, exorcise a demon, or rebuke Satan when she was "loosed from this bond" (verse 16). A synagogue ruler was upset that Jesus healed this woman on the Sabbath, the day of rest (verse 14) but Jesus posed a rhetorical question: "ought not this woman . . . be loosed from this bond on the Sabbath day?" (verse 16). Indeed it was the perfect day of the week for a healing, for one aspect of observing the Sabbath is to remember being released from captivity—"freed." Deuteronomy 5:15 says, "You shall remember that you were a slave in the land of Egypt, and the Lord your God brought you out from there with a might hand and an outstretched arm. Therefore, the Lord your God commanded you to keep the Sabbath."

Paul calls his thorn in the flesh "a messenger of Satan" (2 Corinthians 12:7)—not Satan himself. God is still in charge, as he is the one who gave the thorn in the flesh to Paul. Paul did not rebuke Satan, rather he pleaded with God "that it [not him, namely not Satan] should leave me" (v. 8). We are not sure what Paul's thorn in the flesh was, but it did keep him humble. Because Paul had been so blessed with visionary revelations of Jesus, including his dramatic Damascus road experience, he was at risk of becoming spiritually conceited.

There is one more passage that might imply that the devil is behind physical illness, but it might just apply to demon possession. Of Jesus, Peter said, "He went about doing good and healing all who were oppressed by the devil, for God was with him" (Acts 10:38). The *Anchor Bible Dictionary* comments, "It is significant that summary statements from all 3 [synoptic] gospels (Matthew 4:24; Mark 1:32; and Luke 7:21) list the 'demonized' as a category separate from those suffering with other diseases."

Although the Bible rarely directly attributes physical and mental suffering, other than demon possession, to Satan, the devil may well be active behind the scenes in some physical or mental suffering. I do not, however, think we need to discern just how and when Satan is at work in illness, for this knowledge is not necessary for healing. On the other hand, we should not completely ignore Satan's activity in the world. Behind the scenes, there is an invisible warfare in heaven involving the devil, his demons, and spiritual forces of evil that also affects those of us on earth. Paul says, "Be strong in the Lord and in the strength of his might. Put on the whole armor of God, that you may be able to stand against the schemes of the devil. For we do not wrestle against flesh and blood, but against the rulers, against the authorities, against the cosmic powers over this present darkness, against the spiritual forces of evil in the heavenly places" (Ephesians 6:10–12). Satan may be behind the lies we believe about ourselves and our self-destructive feelings when we are depressed—Satan is known in the Bible for his deceit and his intent on destruction.

Some Christians believe that if a person is depressed, Satan should be rebuked and cast out. Some even try to exorcise demons and evil or unclean spirits from people with mental illness even though there are no places in Scripture where Jesus or his apostles cast out demons from mentally ill people. To rebuke and try to cast out Satan or exorcise demons can be very confusing to depressed people, who are often very suggestible. How can we recognize when Satan and his demons are active in a depressed person and how is he or they active? Do we need to recognize their activity for healing to occur? What does it mean if the person is not healed? Are Satan and his demons still present? What if our depression gets better for a while and then gets worse, often the next morning? Are they back in us again?

Some Christians believe that those who were demon-possessed during the time Jesus and his apostles were on earth were, in fact, mentally ill—maybe schizophrenic. They could not be more mistaken. Those who were mentally ill with schizophrenia could not be so coherent when they identified Jesus as the Son of God and realized what a threat he was to them. For example, when Jesus was in the country of the Gerasene, a demon possessed man who wore no clothes, lived among the tombs, was under guard and was bound with shackles, and who upon seeing Jesus, cried out "What have you to do with me, Jesus, Son of the Most High God? I beg you, do not torment me." A violent schizophrenic simply could not come up with such a coherent question and plea for Jesus to leave him alone with his legion of demons (Luke 8:26 ff.; cf. Mark 5:1 ff.). It is not surprising that demon-possessed people were so common with the inbreaking of the kingdom of God when the God-man, Jesus, reigned on earth. With the combined supernatural and natural presence of God on earth (incarnate from the Holy Spirit and the virgin Mary, and was made man) we would expect for the those from the kingdom of darkness to become more palpably present. Jesus' reign on earth not only brought salvation to mankind, his presence began the destruction of the usually invisible world of evil. As Jesus proclaimed the gospel (good news) of the arrival of the kingdom (of heaven), he healed those "oppressed by demons" (Matthew 4:23 ff.). Those demon-possessed were in a separate category from "all the sick, those afflicted with various diseases and pains . . . those having seizures, and paralytics" (verse 5:24).

It is not surprising that demon possession has become rare these days since Jesus' reign on earth is now invisible. Demons may be active behind the scenes but they are no longer frequently palpably present. I have never seen a single case of demon possession in my forty years of family practice and in my teaching in the United States and Kenya. Palpable demonic activity will come again when Jesus returns to earth (his second coming) to completely destroy the evil kingdom in a final battle between good and evil (Revelation 16: 14).

Many well-meaning Christians may also unknowingly minimize the reality of God's sovereignty over all suffering, including his sovereignty over Job's suffering and Paul's thorn in the flesh. It may be as one biblical scholar has noted that "Satan's greatest deception is to persuade us that we do not need to acknowledge the sovereignty of God."

Some Christians fail to grasp the redemptive aspect of suffering. Over and over again, we are taught in the Bible that God ordains suffering to test us, to strengthen our relationship with him, build up our faith, and better our character. And God will always use the suffering of Christians for their ultimate good, as he did for Joseph in Egypt, when Joseph said to his brothers who had acted sinfully against him, "As for you, you meant evil against me, but God meant it for good" (Genesis 50:20).

Satan is, however, active in some ways behind the scenes. He is "the accuser of our brothers" (Revelation 12:10). In the Lord's law court in heaven in Job 1:6–12, Satan accused Job of fearing God (of trusting God and trying to be obedient to him) because the Lord had blessed Job so much. But Job proved Satan wrong; he continued to trust God despite his great suffering, including severe depression. Trusting God in spite of suffering is one of the main themes of the book of Job.

Thankfully Satan can no longer accuse us in heaven. He has been thrown out of the heavenly courtroom. The Apostle John says there was a war in heaven in which the archangel Michael and his angels defeated the dragon and his angels so that there was no longer any place for them in heaven (Revelation 12:7–8). "The great dragon was thrown down, that ancient serpent, who is called the devil and Satan, the deceiver of the whole world—he was thrown down to the earth, and his angels were thrown down with him . . . 'The accuser of our brothers has been thrown down, who accuses them day and night before God'" (vv. 9–10). It is implicit that this preliminary battle occurred when the Lamb's blood was shed (v. 11). Jesus, the one who died on the cross for our sins, is now risen and ascended and standing in the heavenly courtroom constantly interceding for us. Satan no longer has a case against believers, so there is no place for him in heaven. The devil has been thrown out of the heavenly courtroom, but he is still active in accusing believers on earth: "The devil has come down to you [those on the earth] in great wrath, because he knows that his time is short!" (v. 12).

Among other things, Satan deceives depressed people into thinking that they are worthless and failures. He accuses them of unforgivable sin causing inappropriate guilt. He would have them believe that they should live lives of silent shame. He would have depressed people believe that God is angry with them when it is the devil, himself, who is angry. Satan would have depressed people believe God has abandoned them when, in fact, the Holy Spirit is always present with and within believers. In a limited sense, Satan can be rebuked. Better yet, we should stand with Jesus in the heavenly courtroom and deny that Satan, groveling on the earth, has a case against us.

# 12

## Spiritual Helps for Depression: What We Can Know

HAVING DISCUSSED FOUR SPIRITUAL myths about depression, we now turn to eight spiritual helps for depression. The helps are often appropriate for suffering in general, but are especially helpful in those suffering from depression:

1. Knowing who we are—our dignity and brokenness
2. Realizing depression can be an emotional alarm system
3. Finding meaning in suffering
4. Knowing that God is present in our suffering
5. Remembering God's promises
6. Waiting with hope
7. Keeping the Sabbath
8. Reaching out for healing prayer

In this chapter, we'll look at the first five of the eight spiritual helps that focus on what we can know.

## KNOWING WHO WE ARE—OUR
## DIGNITY AND BROKENNESS

The first spiritual help is knowing who we are. Because we are made in the image of God, we have great dignity in the eyes of God. We read in Genesis 1:26–27: "Then God said, 'Let us make man *in our image*, after our likeness. And let them have *dominion* over the fish of the sea and over the birds of the heavens and over the livestock and over all the earth and over every creeping thing . . .' So God created man *in his own image, in the image of God* he created him; male and female he created them" (emphasis added).

In the ancient Near East during the time the book of Genesis was probably written, "the image of god" meant a very specific thing. In Egypt, only the pharaohs (the kings) were the living images of a god. The fifth word in King Tut's long name is Tutankhamun, which means "the living image of the god Amun." Only the pharaoh was the living image of a god; only the pharaoh was the visible representative of the invisible god. In fact they believed they were divine beings.

In the Bible, ordinary people are living images of God. We, male and female, are all kings and queens. Royalty is democratized; every human being is the visible representative on earth of the invisible Creator King who lives most fully in heaven. We, as creaturely kings and queens, are to extend God's rule, namely God's dominion, over the whole earth, including animal and plant life (Genesis 1:26; see also v. 28).

Genesis 5 says that "When God created man, he made him in the likeness of God" (v. 1). Then "he [Adam] fathered a son in his own likeness, after his image, and named him Seth," and then Adam "had other sons and daughters" (vv. 3–4). To be the living image of God is also to be a son or daughter of God. All the pharaohs, including King Tut, had the phrase "the son of god" in their long names. Luke picks up this idea at the end of his genealogy of Jesus when he lists Jesus' most distant ancestors, namely "the son of Enos, the son of Seth, the son of Adam, the son of God" (Luke 3:38). We are the living images of God—kings and queens who are also sons and daughters of God our great king. We are the royal children of God.

Other people will not always affirm us as persons made in the living image of God; they will not always affirm us as royal sons and daughters of God. In fact, our dignity is frequently undermined by those around us. Sadly, we are sometimes hurt most by those we most care about, sometimes, strangely enough, by those who love us most. Growing up in a home where a child's dignity is undermined can leave lasting emotional scars that can contribute to depression in childhood and later in life. Regardless of the past damage to our sense of dignity, however, we can often be at least partially restored through regularly reminding ourselves of our dignity in the eyes of God. You are "the apple of his [the Lord's] eye" (Deuteronomy 32:10), and "he who touches you touches the apple of his [the Lord's] eye" (Zechariah 2:8). The eye is the most sensitive spot in the human body. God hurts with you whenever people hurt you. He will never hurt you the way some people may have hurt you in your life.

We were supposed to be priestly kings. Moses says that Israel was to be "a kingdom of priests and a holy nation" (Exodus 19:6). Before his fall in the garden of Eden, Adam was a godly priest-king. Genesis 2:15 says "The Lord God took the man and put him in the garden of Eden to work it and keep it." We cannot go into all the reasons the garden of Eden was the palace temple of God, but when the words *work* (= serve) and *keep* (= guard) are used together elsewhere in the Old Testament, they refer to the work of the priests serving in and guarding the tabernacle or temple.

Unfortunately, we priest-kings often exercise our dominion in unholy ways. Some depressed people have been hurt by parents who exercised their authority over them in dominating, demeaning ways. Some depressed people have been hurt by spouses who have abused their power and victimized them. At a societal level, the powerful accumulate wealth at the expense of the poor, who live lives of quiet desperation. In some parts of the world there is the daily stress of people not knowing whether their roof will leak tonight or whether they will eat tomorrow. The impoverished have higher rates of depression.

Even after the fall of humankind in Adam as recorded in Genesis 3, we are still God's living images on earth—his royal sons and daughters—and he is very protective of us. He ordains capital punishment for those who commit first-degree murder—those who intentionally destroy his image (Genesis 9:6). When we are defiled or damaged by others, God is furious at those who have hurt us; and he loves us, his royal children, even more. In his eyes, we are not the damaged goods we think we are.

But in our own eyes, we are damaged goods—broken. Our self-image has been shattered, broken into many pieces. This brokenness is manifested, in part, in our many weaknesses as human beings, including the tendency of some to depression. Depressed people cannot imagine how all the pieces can be put back to together, how their wholeness (shalom) can be restored. Even less can they imagine that God will re-create them into an even better image of himself than their original one. In fact, in one very important sense, we are already new creatures in Christ, though it may not feel like it. Paul says, "If anyone is in Christ, he is a new creation. The old [flesh] has passed away; behold, the new has come" (2 Corinthians 5:17). When we feel broken, we need to remind ourselves of who we are in Christ, a new creation, regardless of how we feel. We are daily being re-created in Christ, who is the perfect image of God. "He [Jesus] is the image of the invisible God, the firstborn of creation" (Colossians 1:15).

It may seem odd to think that recognizing that we are broken and weak is a spiritual "help," but it is.

First, God knows our brokenness and weaknesses and accepts us as we are, so we don't need to pretend to ourselves and others that we aren't broken and that we don't have weaknesses. A burden may be lifted a little bit from your shoulders just by being transparent to yourself and others.

Second, God often strengthens us in our weaknesses. In 2 Corinthians 12:9–10, the Lord said to Paul, "My grace is sufficient for you, for my power is made perfect in weakness"; Paul said in response, "I am content with weaknesses . . . For when I am weak, then I am strong." God often uses our weaknesses to bring himself more honor and glory (the honor and glory he desires) by strengthening us through his grace and power.

Third, we are told in the Bible that God will heal those who are broken, including those suffering mentally. King David says of the righteous [those who try to trust and obey the Lord], "The Lord is near to the brokenhearted and saves *the crushed in spirit*" (Psalm 34:18—emphasis mine). He also says of God regarding the outcasts and afflicted, "He heals the brokenhearted and binds up their wounds" (Psalm 147:3). Isaiah prophesied regarding the coming Messiah, "He has sent me to bind up the brokenhearted . . . to comfort all who mourn; to grant to those who mourn in Zion—to give them a beautiful headdress instead of ashes, the oil of gladness instead of mourning, the garment of praise instead of *a faint spirit*" (Isaiah 61:1–3, emphasis mine).

Jesus will bring about a radical redemptive reversal for those who are brokenhearted, those who mourn, those who have a faint (weak) spirit. He will bring gladness and praise. This reversal may begin in this life, but its fullness must wait until the consummation of all things, the day of Christ's second coming. Severely depressed people do not experience this gladness or a spirit uplifted with praise. But Jesus will eventually bring this healing to even the most severely depressed people, though it may take weeks, months, even years. Sadly, for a small minority of depressed people, this reversal will not come until their resurrected life in heaven.

> Dear Lord, I'm regularly confronted with my brokenness. People have hurt me, and I've also embraced harmful lies about who I am. I recognize that even though my brokenness can be painful, you are using it to help me realize my weakness and my great

*need for you. In fact, you said that your power is made perfect in
weakness.*

*I'm so grateful that I can be real with you about my broken-
ness and frailty, and you don't look down on me. What a comfort
it is to know that you understand and will bring complete healing one day! You will create beauty from these ashes. When I feel
broken beyond repair, please remind me of the good news that you
have already made me new! I am part of your royal family! Since
I bear your image, I have great dignity. I ask that you bring this
thought to my troubled mind regularly and use it to foster healing. In Jesus' name I pray, Amen.*

## REALIZING THAT DEPRESSION CAN BE
## AN EMOTIONAL ALARM SYSTEM

The second spiritual help is realizing that depression can be an emotional
alarm system. A substantial part of this section is my reflection on this topic
from Gary Lovejoy's *Light in the Darkness* (see Selective Bibliography). A
devoted Christian counselor and professor of psychology and religion,
Lovejoy coauthors this book with a family physician. Lovejoy believes depression is an alarm system that is built in by God. While the difference is
subtle, I believe that depression is primarily a manifestation of our brokenness. However, I also believe that the idea of an emotional alarm system can
help depressed people see how God can use their depression to bring about
needed change.

God uses our depression like an alarm system—like the flashing lights
and ear-piercing sounds from an ambulance rushing to the hospital with a
physically broken person after a car accident. Because depression is so painful, it may be effective in getting us to pay attention to personal problems we
have neglected. Depression may be a wake-up call to recognize and/or do
something about disordered relationships with God and/or with one's fellow man, including those closest to us. It may prompt us to address relationship conflicts that we have been ignoring or we have been too afraid to deal
with. Depression can also nudge us to clear away the baggage we carry from
a troubled past, including resentments, fears, and self-hatred. When things
fall apart, depression is your chance to begin to rearrange the broken pieces.

Consider the example of resentment and unforgiveness. Martin Lu-
ther King Jr. once said, "Refusal to forgive is a poison you take hoping it
will destroy your enemy." Instead of hurting your enemy, unforgiveness can
become self-destructive. The book of Hebrews refers to a "root of bitterness"

that "springs up and causes trouble, and by it many become defiled" (Hebrews 12:15). The Apostle John says, "Whoever loves God must also love his brother" (1 John 4:20–21). These are strong words, but God really wants us to work on any unforgiveness we harbor in our hearts. Forgiveness often helps resolve bitterness and resentment and in turn lessens the severity of the depression. The Apostle Paul exhorts us to be "tenderhearted, forgiving one another, as God in Christ forgave you" (Ephesians 4:32). Our usual sinful reflex to being wronged is revenge, but this is not the way God wants us to handle being wronged.

How can we recognize the alarm of resentment and anger and reach toward forgiveness? Proverbs 19:11 advises that we "overlook an offense." Sometimes we just need to let go of a wrong done to us. And 1 Peter 4:8 notes that "love covers a multitude of sins." In other words, we need to keep short accounts of the wrongs done to us by others. In his model prayer, the Lord Jesus ties our Father's forgiveness of our sins to our forgiving those who have sinned against us (Matthew 6:14). There is a requirement for us to forgive in order to be forgiven by our Father.

If we can't put the offense to rest or it is a more serious offense that needs to be addressed, then we need to consider talking lovingly with the person who offended us. If talking with someone one-on-one doesn't resolve the problem, Jesus says in a somewhat different context, "take one or two others along with you" (Matthew 18:16). A depressed person may not have the emotional strength, or may be too emotionally unstable, to go to the offending party alone. In that case, going with another supportive and wise person from the start may be needed. A counselor can help the offended party determine, and even rehearse, what he/she will say during the meeting with the offender. Counselors might also bring the two people in conflict together in an office setting to help the two parties be less defensive or caustic and more conciliatory.

When we are wrongfully offended and no amends have been made after talking with the person who has offended us, we should never take revenge. Paul says, "Repay no one evil for evil . . . never avenge yourself . . . overcome evil with good" (Romans 12:17–21). Showing goodness can be healing to us even if the offending person spurns the good will. When nothing works to resolve a personal offense, we need to leave justice to God. Paul says in regards to someone who had done him great harm, "the Lord will repay him according to his deeds" (2 Timothy 4:14). We need to leave retributive justice to God.

Depression is often rightly described as "dark" or "darkness," but depression may actually shine a light on some parts of our thinking, speaking, or acting. More seriously depressed people may not be able to see these things in a proper light or, if they do, they may not be able to do much to effect change at first. But as their depressions lift, the alarm system helps them see what needs to be worked on and may help motivate them to address those problematic areas, often with the help of a counselor or clergy.

Seriously depressed people may not be able to see any good resulting from their depressions. But over time God can use our depressions to make us better people. If, as you begin to improve from clinical depression, you continue self-condemning rumination or helpless resignation, you may doom yourself to a world bereft of options to do something different—to draw yourself a better tomorrow. If you let him, God will never waste an experience, even a painful one, though it may take a long time before you see how God has healed you, at least in part, from your brokenness.

> Lord God, depression is terrible, but I believe that you can use it to get my attention—like an emotional alarm system. I see that the pain can alert me to problems in my relationship with you and with the people I know and love. You can work through this darkness to shine a light on any dysfunctional patterns in the way that I think, act, or speak. May the heaviness prompt me to let go of destructive baggage from my past that weighs me down with resentment and fear. I want to move beyond self-condemnation and resignation to a place of lighthearted freedom and unshakable trust in you, my powerful Redeemer. Thank you for determining to use all this for your glory and my good.

## FINDING MEANING IN SUFFERING

The third spiritual help is finding meaning in suffering. Depressed people may feel that life is meaningless. They may not even remember that they once felt life was meaningful. They may see no purpose in their suffering; their life doesn't seem to matter to anyone, including God.

We need meaning in life to survive and thrive. The book *Man's Search for Meaning* was written by Victor Frankl, a Jewish psychoanalyst who survived German incarceration, brutal labor, and starvation during the Holocaust. He studied the morbidity and mortality of fellow concentration camp victims. Frankl found that those who believed that there was meaning in life in spite of their suffering were healthier mentally and were less likely to become physically sick or die. The common experience of pain and love for one another grounded those who found meaning in suffering. Without the experience of love, life rapidly becomes meaningless.

Suffering does have meaning. For example, the Apostle Paul says, "Suffering produces endurance, and endurance produces character, and character produces hope" (Romans 5:3–4). There is meaning in our suffering, but it is a hard pill to swallow. There is nothing easy about the sequence of suffering, endurance, character, and hope. However, the sequence really does helps us mature in the Christian faith.

Suffering people need to see how their story is part of a bigger story, that their painful personal story is connected to a larger meaningful story. They need to believe they are a part of the greatest narrative of all—the true story of God in Christ and his beloved people. Even the torment of depression is a part of a bigger story that includes Jesus' agony in the garden of Gethsemane and on the cross.

A sense of meaninglessness is not only a result of depression; it may be a contributor as well. Qoholet, the wise author of the book of Ecclesiastes, purposely tried many different things that he thought might bring him meaning in life: excessive drinking, constructing great buildings and gardens, hoarding possessions, and creating a harem. However, he discovered that only the fear of the Lord (trusting God and trying to be obedient to his gracious instruction) and a simple lifestyle bring meaning to life. In the second-to-the-last verse, Qoholet says, "Fear God and keep his commandments, for this is the whole duty of man" (Ecclesiastes 12:13). Fearing God is a deep reverence for the Lord—an abiding trust in him and a strong commitment to living out his plan for our lives by following his gracious commandments.

It is not surprising to most Christians that we need to fear God in this sense, but Qoholet also says that some very mundane things in our daily life—such as enjoying eating and drinking and finding satisfaction in work—bring meaning. In Ecclesiastes 2:24, we read, "There is nothing better for a person than that he should eat and drink and find enjoyment in his toil. This also, I saw, is from the hand of God." I believe a simple lifestyle will help prevent and relieve depression caused by burnout. Unfortunately, in the midst of depression, people often do not enjoy the simple things in life, such as food and drink, and they may be unable to find satisfaction in work, if they are able to work at all. If the lack of satisfying work is contributing to a mild or moderate depression, you may, at some point, need to look for a more meaningful job.

Meaningful activities often slip away in depression. If this is the case with you, these activities need to be gradually reintroduced. If photography used to bring meaning to your life, push yourself to do it again. Starting with just one photograph of a dog you love may help bring a little meaning to your life. You may even be able to push yourself to post it on Facebook.

Meaningful activities may have been lacking before depression. In that case, new meaningful activities may need to be gradually introduced. Take up gardening and try to commit to it at least five minutes each day. Maybe write a one-sentence thank you note to a supportive friend: "Thank you for being my friend during this hard time for me."

> *Lord Jesus, please help me to believe that my suffering will produce greater maturity and yield something good that can benefit others. Even you had to endure suffering, but it achieved amazing things for the entire world! Though my life can feel meaningless, I know that I am connected to you, the Source of All Meaning! Enable me to fully embrace the hope I have in you. I also ask that you'll empower me to take steps in the right direction—accomplishing little activities that used to brighten my day; maybe they will eventually brighten my day again. Please protect me from believing the lie that my efforts don't matter. You are the One who fills each moment with significance—even when I can't see it. Remind me that my life is part of a bigger story that has a happy ending. I want to experience your love while finding purpose and enjoyment in a simple lifestyle. May these struggles cause me to revere you more deeply and obey you more fully.*

## KNOWING THAT GOD IS PRESENT IN OUR SUFFERING

The prophet Isaiah says of the Lord regarding his redeemed people, "When you pass through the waters, I will be with you; and through the rivers, they shall not overwhelm you; when you walk through fire you shall not be burned, and the flame shall not consume you" (Isaiah 43:2). The author of the book of Hebrews reminds the young persecuted church that God had said, "I will never leave you nor forsake you" (Hebrews 13:5). The very last thing Jesus said on earth was "I am with you always, to the end of the age" (Matthew 28:20). Paul says of those justified through Christ Jesus' death and resurrection, "Who shall separate us from the love of Christ? Shall tribulation, or distress, or persecution, or famine, or nakedness, or danger, or sword? . . . I am sure that neither death nor life, nor angels nor rulers, nor things present nor things to come, nor powers, nor height nor depth, nor anything else in all creation, will be able to separate us from the love of God in Christ Jesus our Lord" (Romans 8:35, 38–39). When we are at our worst and weakest, God is still with us, and we need to listen to his voice (including meditating on Scripture and praying—see Appendices C and D) in the midst of our pain.

It is also reassuring to know that God knows what abandonment feels like; he has experienced the suffering of abandonment. On the cross, Jesus cried out, "My God, my God, why have you forsaken me?" (Matthew 27:46). The background of Jesus' words is Psalm 22:1-2. King David cried out to God, "My God, my God, why have you forsaken me? Why are you so far from saving me, from the words of my groaning? O my God, I cry by day, but you do not answer, and by night, but I find no rest." David felt abandoned, but he was not. Later in the same psalm (vv. 24-25), David praises the God who has heard his cries, "For he has not despised or abhorred the affliction of the afflicted, and he has not hidden his face from him, but has heard, when he cried to him. From you comes my praise in the great congregation."

Jesus, on the other hand, was truly abandoned by God the Father who could not look at the mountainous load of sin his Son was bearing on the cross. The prophet Habakkuk said of the Lord, "Your eyes are too pure to look on evil; you cannot tolerate wrong" (Habakkuk 1:13, NIV). Because Jesus was forsaken by the Father on our behalf, we will never be forsaken as Jesus was.

God is always present in our suffering, though depressed people may find it hard to believe. They often do not feel God's presence. They ask questions like, where is the evidence that God loves me? If God is present, why don't I feel it? Often, we do not understand why God allows us to suffer, but we do know from the garden of Gethsemane and Jesus' crucifixion that he fully understands and feels our suffering.

Fortunately, suffering is not God's ultimate plan for our life. It is not God's final word. In the new heaven and new earth, when God makes his dwelling place with humanity, just as Jesus made his dwelling place with humanity when he was on earth (John 1:14), "He will wipe away every tear from their eyes, and death shall be no more, neither shall there be mourning, nor crying, nor pain anymore, for the former things have passed away" (Revelation 21:4).

Our glory is God's plan for our future. Paul says, "The sufferings of this present time are not worth comparing with the glory that will be revealed in us" (Romans 8:18). Paul is not trying to minimize suffering, but he does want us to know that, by comparison, today's suffering is more than reversed by the abundant, eternal life we will have with God. When I am severely depressed, often my only hope is in the abundant, eternal life to come in heaven.

> *My Savior, thank you for being with me every step of this painful journey. You are no stranger to suffering, and the path of crucifixion that you walked through was more excruciating than I*

*can fathom. You understand how I feel better than anyone else.
Because of your suffering, I will eventually be free from my suffering. Not only that, but even now, you are working through my
suffering to bring me future glory. Please generate in me an eternal
mind-set that is focused on when there will be no more suffering.
Help me to fix my thoughts on the glorious reality that awaits me
in heaven. During the dark times, may this perspective provide
the strength and perseverance I need to keep living in light of the
truth.*

## REMEMBERING GOD'S PROMISES

The fifth spiritual help is remembering God's promises when we are depressed. So much of the self-talk depressed people engage in is demoralizing. Everything looks bad, and we believe that the bad will invariably get
worse. Sometimes we can't help thinking this way, but we should try to
replace negative self-talk with helpful, truthful self-talk.

Michelle Bengtson rightly emphasizes the need to replace negative
self-talk with God's biblical promises. Her book *Hope Prevails* is filled with
reminders of helpful verses that can be useful in dealing with all kinds of
negative self-talk. For example, many scriptural passages remind us that the
Lord will heal those who suffer. A verse we looked at earlier says that the
Lord "heals the brokenhearted and binds up their wounds" (Psalm 147:3).
Many other verses remind us that the Lord is near us in our suffering; he has
not abandoned us. (In Appendix C, I have suggested many biblical passages
of healing and hope.)

I do not find "claiming" God's promises to be helpful. It sounds too
much like winning a door prize and being able to claim it immediately. It
sounds as if we are confident that we will benefit from the promise exactly
as we want when we want. "Remembering" is a more biblical concept than
"claiming." In *Young's Analytical Concordance* there are more than 200
verses that include the word *remembering* and none for *claiming*. For most
depressed people, remembering good things, such as God's promises, is not
a passive activity of the mind. We need to actively remind ourselves of God's
promises and be willing to wait to see how and when he will fulfill them.
Remember that old hymn "Standing on the Promises"? The second verse
reads, "Standing on the promises I cannot fail, / When the howling storms
of doubt and fear assail, / By the living word of God I shall prevail, / Standing on the promises of God."

Sometimes quoting God's promises is misused by those counseling depressed people. For example, Romans 8:28 says "that for those who love God all things work together for good." At some point in time, maybe not until heaven, this is true for all Christians. But some who counsel imply by quoting this promise that because God works all things out for good, you should stop feeling depressed now.

> *Heavenly Father, sometimes my mind gets stuck in a negative rut—evaluating myself and my circumstances through the worst possible lens. Please help me to replace my defeating, demoralizing self-talk with uplifting promises found in the Bible. I recognize that it is vitally important for me to find nourishment in your life-giving Word instead of feeding on harmful accusations and speculations. Enable me to be intentional about remembering your promises—especially when I'm being pulled into old ways of thinking. As I consider your promises, keep me from a demanding, presumptuous attitude. May I hold each promise with humility— understanding that only you know when and how it will unfold in my life. I ask all this in Jesus' name, Amen.*

# 13

## Spiritual Helps for Depression: What We Can Do

WE'VE LOOKED AT FIVE spiritual helps that address what we can know. There are three more spiritual helps that address what we can do: waiting with hope, keeping the Sabbath, seeking out healing prayer.

### WAITING WITH HOPE

The sixth spiritual help is waiting with hope. There is a single Hebrew word that is sometimes best translated as "wait" and other times as "hope." Combining these two translations, we come up with the concept of "waiting with hope"—both meanings are a part of one Hebrew word.

From depressed Jeremiah's biblical book of Lamentations, we previously noted that he said, "My soul is bereft of peace; I have forgotten what happiness is; so I say, 'My endurance has perished; so has my hope from the Lord'" (Lamentations 3:17–18). Just three verses later, however, Jeremiah says, "But this I call to mind, and therefore have hope: The steadfast love of the Lord never ceases; his mercies never come to an end; they are new every morning; great is your faithfulness. 'The Lord is my portion,' says my soul, 'therefore I will hope in him'" (vv. 21–24).

First, Jeremiah says that his hope from the Lord has perished, but then he says that he will hope in the Lord. It sounds as if Jeremiah is talking himself into waiting with hope (an early example of cognitive-behavioral therapy, which we discussed earlier). Jeremiah acknowledges his misperception about God—the perception that God will never bring him peace or happiness. And he replaces this misperception with evidence-based alternative thoughts such as "the steadfast love of the Lord never ceases" and "great is your faithfulness." Job says, even while he is deep in depression, "Though he [God] slay me, I will hope in him" (Job 13:15). This verse appears in my tombstone epitaph. (Remember, my wife and I ordered our tombstone when I was dying from terminal cancer.) Job had lost everything. The only thing that was not taken from him was his life and his wife—the latter who early on in his suffering tried to make him cynical. Even Job's friends unknowingly worsened his suffering. Despite this, somehow Job was able to wait with hope for God's deliverance. The past influences our present state of mind, but so does anticipating a hopeful future.

Isaiah brings hope to those who feel as if the Lord is not watching over them:

> Have you not known? Have you not heard? The Lord is the everlasting God, the Creator of the ends of the earth. He does not faint or grow weary; his understanding is unsearchable. He gives power to the faint, and to him who has no might he increases strength. Even youths shall faint and be weary, and young men shall fall exhausted; but they who wait for the Lord shall renew their strength; they shall mount up like eagles; they shall run and not be weary; they shall walk and not faint. (Isaiah 40:28–31)

Waiting with hope during suffering requires endurance and a steadfast trust in God. Endurance is not a popular concept today. Nobody wants to wait for anything, especially healing from suffering. Endurance is a spiritual discipline in my way of thinking, but it is for the most part a lost spiritual discipline. In contrast, the Bible places real value on endurance and steadfastness. Jesus' brother James says, "The testing of your faith produces steadfastness. And let steadfastness have its full effect, that you may be perfect and complete" (James 1:2–3). To become perfect and complete, *shalom* in Hebrew, often requires endurance. Endurance will not only result in our personal betterment; it will also make us more empathetic and compassionate toward others. In 2 Corinthians 1:4, Paul says the "God of all comfort . . . comforts us in all our affliction, so that we may be able to comfort those who are in any affliction, with the comfort with which we ourselves are comforted by God."

Unfortunately, some people think that enduring is all that we should do about our suffering, that is, we should just accept our depression. God does permit us to suffer, but he also wants us to seek healing, directly from himself but also through his providential care. God is at work in all of his creation all of the time. Jesus says of his Father in heaven, "He makes his sun rise on the evil and on the good, and sends rain on the just and on the unjust" (Matthew 5:45). Jesus uses this saying to encourage us to love everyone, but it implicitly recognizes God's providential care of everyone. God does many good things for all people, not just believers.

Oddly, some depressed Christians don't seek the healing care that God provides to people through medical care and counseling. It is not being more spiritual to ignore these helps. God has given these means of common grace to heal us. Depressed Christians should, of course, seek relief from their suffering through the special grace of spiritual care as well, maybe from a clergyperson. To ignore these means of common and special grace is to our detriment. It also robs God of some of the glory he can gain for himself through healing us.

Severely depressed people can become utterly hopeless through no fault of their own. It is usually the result of severe and prolonged mental suffering. Thinking about hope and praying for hope does not always bring hope. But even trying to be hopeful may help. Try to hope for hope if that is all the hope you can muster. Sadly, in the severely depressed, hopelessness can reach the point where they consider suicide. The painful burden of life seems too great to bear for what they believe will be the rest of their life. With a psychiatrist, I had been co-managing a depressed, older, Christian woman for several years, and she never improved. One cold winter night she got up from bed, put on her robe and slippers, and walked into the freezing pond in her backyard, taking her own life. I was devastated. All that we had to give her was not enough.

When you are depressed remind yourself that "Those who sow in tears shall reap with shouts of joy! He who goes out weeping, bearing the seed for sowing, shall come home with shouts of joy, bringing his sheaves with him" (Psalm 126:5–6). In the metaphor of sowing and reaping, it takes half a year for those who sow in tears to reap with shouts of joy. When you are desperate for relief, remember that it may take a metaphorical six months to reap what you have sown. In my case, it took years, but it did come. It usually does not take that long.

Suicide in a severely depressed person usually does not have anything to do with selfishness or revenge toward other people or rebellion against God or any other commonly suspect motives. Suicide is usually the final result of complete hopelessness that comes with seemingly endless mental torment and despair. It is a great tragedy, not selfishness, revenge, or rebellion.

Suicide is, of course, also a great tragedy for those left behind. It often leaves wounds that never completely heal. If you are thinking about suicide, please don't go through with it. I know your pain—as previously noted, I once tried to commit suicide. Please, please try to endure and reach out for help—reach out for help right now. If you don't know where to turn for help call the National Suicide Prevention Lifeline at 800-273-8255, open 24/7.

> *My Lord, this mental anguish has gone on for so long, and I am weary to the bone. I just want to give up—especially when I think that there is no chance of improvement. Please give me your strength . . . strength to endure . . . strength to keep trying to hope that there is hope. In this desolate season, I want to envision and anticipate a bright future where life is vibrant and joyful again. I know that pressing on through this trial with endurance can help me to grow. It will also make me more empathic and compassionate toward those who are suffering. Please enable me to wait on you and trust that you will renew my strength and give me hope.*

## KEEPING THE SABBATH

The seventh spiritual help is keeping the Sabbath. God was the first to celebrate the Sabbath. God's Sabbath rest (Genesis 2:1–3) began with his enthronement above his creation with his feet reaching down to the earth on the last day of creation. The Lord says in Isaiah 66:1, "Heaven is my throne, and the earth is my footstool."

Ancient Near Eastern kings were said to "rest" after victory in battle by building a palace for themselves and a temple for their gods. God, the great creator king, was restfully satisfied on the seventh day with his combined palace and temple that is creation—he is both King and the only God. The visible heavens and the earth are not merely the environment in which humanity lives, they are also the dwelling place of God.

We are told that God, in addition to resting on the seventh day of creation, was refreshed: "On the seventh day he rested and was refreshed" (Exodus 31:17). The word *refresh* is a Hebrew verbal form of the noun *nephesh*, or "living being," that we noted in regard to Adam. God's own being was enlivened by his creative work, and he continues to refreshingly enjoy his creation, especially "living beings" who love and trust in him.

God's Sabbath rest didn't end after the seventh day of creation. It is endless. Hebrews 4:1 says, "The promise of entering his rest still stands," so God's rest is ongoing. There is an aspect of God's rest that we can participate in now. Hebrews 4:3 refers to "we who have believed enter that rest." When we celebrate the Sabbath, we join in God's restful refreshment.

After delivering the Israelites from oppressive enslavement by the Egyptians, God graciously gave the Israelites the Ten Commandments, which included regular Sabbath observance. Exodus 20:8–11 (the fourth of the Ten Commandments) ties our keeping the Sabbath with the Lord who "rested on the seventh day." His celebration of Sabbath is the model for ours. In Sabbath rest and refreshment, we are worshiping God as king and delighting with him in his creation palace temple, of which we, his royal children, are a part. Every Sabbath we, his creaturely kings and queens, should reenact the enthronement of God in creation.

Every Sabbath is a celebration. Sabbath observance is not to be a set of unpleasant, legalistic responsibilities. Rather, it should include activities that bring rest and refreshment. It should, of course, include the regular worship of God. Even depressed people can participate in worship; some may even get some relief, if not joy, from worship. Often, I have received brief relief from depression during worship. Worshiping God with fellow believers promotes a deeper relationship with God and with our brothers and sisters in Christ. As we have seen from interpersonal therapy, healthy relationships are important for preventing and treating depression.

Every seventh day is to be a holy day, meaning it is to be set apart for God's use. Every Sabbath is to be a regular time set apart for satisfying rest from the labor of the previous week and refreshment for the week to come. God has made us such that we need regular days of rest and refreshment.

Modern life is just too hectic, often leaving us unable to cope with stress. I believe this weekly day of rest and refreshment will renew our strength—maybe bringing healing from or prevention of depression; if we are on a treadmill, keeping the Sabbath may help us get off the treadmill.

Part of the reason we may be dissatisfied with the previous week's work is that we feel that we have not done enough. We feel we need to do more. So we spend part of our Sabbath doing more of the work that we need to rest from. This work may be for self-centered reasons, but alternatively, it may be that we think we need to do more for the kingdom of God; we don't recognize that resting and refreshing ourselves on the Sabbath is "doing more." Resting and refreshing is exactly what God wants us to do. He wants us to imitate him celebrating the Sabbath. If God is king in our lives, we need to be obedient to his commands—commands that, after all, are for our good. We need to let him apportion us work for each of the weekly six days of work and apportion us rest and refreshment for the seventh. For ideas on how to celebrate the Sabbath, read Keeping the Sabbath Wholly, by Marva Dawn. It is not a series of do's and don'ts. It is a handbook of pleasures to be experienced and share with others on the Sabbath.

Once we have started to keep the Sabbath, we can try to bring little bits of the Sabbath into every day of the week. Someone who reviewed my book asked me how I bring in bits of the Sabbath into everyday life. I will share how I do this at this time in my life without at all implying that how I do it is how you should do it. In fact, because I now work half-time in medicine, I can devote more time to my devotions than can most people who work full time. Maybe, however, sharing my approach will give you some ideas about how to improve your devotional life if it is lagging.

I take time most days when I first get up to read and meditate on God's Word. I am also in a Bible study with three other people. I use the help of a study Bible or a commentary and slowly go through the passage over the course of a week. I meditate on one or more verses I have studied. I also meditate on the writings of Christian authors from all ages. Currently I am meditating on Puritan prayers and devotions from *The Valley of Vision*. Just before that, I slowly, delightfully made my way through the new edition of *The Book of Common Prayer*—everything in the Anglican liturgy is directly based on the teachings of the Bible. My wife loves *Jesus Calling*.

I'm sure there are many ways to meditate, but I'll share one way I do it. I currently slowly read a Puritan prayer or devotion three times and then settle on a line or two. I try to make those lines applicable to myself, especially in my relationship with Jesus. Sometimes I do the same with a Psalm.

I made a serious attempt to really meditate only after my healing from metastatic cancer and depression five years ago. At first, I found it extremely hard to do. I have always been able to read and digest material quickly, but true meditation took many months before I got any benefit at all. I continued the spiritual discipline only because I had read the writings of trustworthy Christian authors who found it very helpful. Even now, I am just a novice at meditation, but I find it invaluable in my walk with Christ. Some things I had read about meditation encouraged me to empty my mind and let it fill with what sounds like an almost supernatural presence of Jesus. In the six months I did this daily, I never once was able to truly empty my mind or feel anything that felt supernatural. Many thoughts with little meaning always floated through my mind serving only to distract me. Obviously, this is not a gift that the Holy Spirit has given to me. Praying through the Psalms, as noted above, has been more helpful to me. Of course, for most severely depressed people my devotional life is far too much of a reach. Maybe you can just linger on one Scripture verse from Appendix C and one prayer from Appendix D. Maybe you can pray for one of the people who has been of help to you and someone else suffering like you.

The last portion of my devotional life is intercessory prayer. I find that I need to be a part of God's plan for the lives of other people by praying for them. I have so many people I care about (in truth, I have trouble caring about some, but God has impressed on me to pray for them regardless) that I have two prayer lists. Some people I pray for only once a week. Some I pray for daily. People often move back and forth from one list to another. Of course, my wife and children are always on my daily list. People I know who are suffering from depression are always on my daily prayer list. Of course, each day brings some new things that need to prayed for just once.

> *Lord God, initiator and keeper of the Sabbath, sometimes I'm driven to keep on working—whether out of a sense of the need to do more for God or to fulfill my own agenda. However, you have designed me, and you say that I need to implement a weekly rhythm of rest and refreshment. Please help me to set aside work one day a week so that I can worship you with other believers and receive refreshment and renewal on a regular basis. I want to enter into your rest both externally and internally . . . trusting in your finished work, Jesus. May my belief in you ease the pressures and rigors of daily life. I also want to spend time with you each day so that I can enjoy a life-giving oasis of rest more frequently. I believe this will infuse me with your strength . . . enabling me to better cope with the stress in my life. I'm beginning to see that rest actually accomplishes a lot—and the benefits are profound! Thank you for the gift of rest!*

## REACHING OUT FOR HEALING PRAYER

The eighth spiritual help is healing prayer. The prophets knew whom to go to for healing. Jeremiah prayed, "Heal me, O Lord, and I shall be healed; save me and I shall be saved, for you are my praise" (Jeremiah 17:14).

## Biblical Background

As Jesus inaugurated the kingdom of heaven on earth, he healed many: "And Jesus went throughout all the cities and villages, teaching in the synagogues and proclaiming the gospel of the kingdom and healing every disease and every affliction" (Matthew 9:35). The healing kingdom of heaven was breaking into the broken kingdom of this world. Jesus' healings were not only wonderful works of compassion, but also demonstrations of his power and authority. Jesus' healings while he was on earth were categorically different from healings we see today. Jesus' miracles were qualitatively different. With Jesus, the crippled from birth walked and the blind from birth could see. The deaf and mute from birth could hear and speak. A dead man, Lazarus, was raised up from the dead. Jesus waited for two days to come to Lazarus's sisters after he died (John 11), just to make sure that Lazarus was bloating and smelling before he raised him from the dead.

Jesus' frequent miraculous, dramatic healings were evidence that he is the Son of God and that he brings the kingdom of heaven with him to earth. They are evidence that he had the authority to proclaim the authoritative gospel and that we should listen to his gospel as God's Word.

In Luke 9:1-2, Jesus "called the twelve together and gave them power and authority over all demons and to cure diseases, and he sent them out to proclaim the kingdom of God and to heal." The apostles were Jesus' authorized ambassadors in proclaiming the kingdom of God and were given power to miraculously, dramatically heal. They, too, were motivated by compassion for those in the broken kingdom of this world. But their healing was also a testimony to the version of the kingdom of God that Jesus had authorized and that they were now proclaiming as his ambassadors.

We read in Acts that miraculous, dramatic healing power continued to be with the apostles after Jesus died, though we do not see reports of healings nearly as frequently as in the Gospels. The apostles of Jesus, who had been with Jesus for three years during which they personally heard him proclaim his gospel and witnessed his death and resurrection, continued to performed miraculous, dramatic healings. Again, the healings were wonderful works of compassion but also demonstrations of God's supernatural power in the apostles. This power was a witness that the apostles' testimonies are authoritative. The gospel of the kingdom of God proclaimed and lived out by Jesus is the gospel that the apostles proclaimed and we should listen to it as the authoritative Word of God. For their testimony, from reliable tradition, we believe that almost all of the apostles were martyred. It has been rightly said that rarely will a man willingly die for the truth; none will willingly die for a lie.

Paul was an apostle because he had seen and talked with the risen Christ in extraordinarily real visions. He was given extraordinary healing powers to demonstrate that he too was an apostle—an authoritative witness of Jesus. "God was doing extraordinary miracles [of healing] by the hands of Paul" (Acts 19:11). Of himself, Paul said, "The signs of a true apostle were performed among you with utmost patience, with signs and wonders and mighty works" (2 Corinthians 12:12). Paul's miracles were qualitatively different from the "miracles" of the "super-apostles" (v. 11). Paul uses the term *super-apostles* ironically. They considered themselves to be super-apostles, and maybe the members of the Corinthian church did too. But God marked out Paul as a true apostle with full apostolic authority by his qualitatively different miracles, which included "signs and wonders and mighty works," of the sort that consistently in the Bible refer to clearly supernatural events, including supernatural healing. The super-apostles did not work similar signs and wonders and mighty works, nor did they proclaim the same gospel (2 Corinthians 11:4).

## Here and Now

Jesus wants us to continue his healing ministry today through healing prayer. I myself was miraculously healed from metastatic kidney cancer. But even this healing was qualitatively less dramatic that the healings of Jesus and the apostles. The enlarged lymph nodes in my abdomen and thorax could have been due (though it is unlikely) to a different medical disease that spontaneously resolved just before surgery. That was the theory of one of my colleagues. There was never any question when Jesus or his apostles performed a miraculous, dramatic healing.

As a family physician, I know that most healings that people say are miraculous can be explained, at least in part, by God-ordained natural healing processes or God-directed medical interventions. Most of the time physical and mental healing is accomplished, at least in part, by God's providential care through ordinary medical treatment and/or counseling.

Often our prayers for physical and mental healing are not answered in the way that we think they should be. And always remember that when you pray that God will answer your prayer for healing, he may answer with a "yes" or a "no," or a "it is not for you to know at this time if I will heal you in the way you have prayed for; trust me to heal you when and how I decide."

Often healing comes as a sort of cumulative effect over time. This is especially true of depression. We may notice hardly a difference from hour to hour or day to day, but over weeks, months, or years, the healing becomes apparent.

How we pray for healing is also important. It is important to pray in humble trust. We should never pray with presumption. We simply do not know how and when God will heal us, and God will not be manipulated by presumptuous healing prayer. I've heard a Christian healer say that when we pray for healing, we should not include "if it is according your will" since it is always God's will that we be healed. The Bible says the opposite. "Confidence" in prayer should include "if we ask anything *according to his will* he hears us" (1 John 5:14, emphasis added). This type of confidence is not presumptive.

Regardless of whether our prayers are answered in part by medical treatment and/or counseling, healing prayer helps us become a part of God's numerous providential healings and occasional miraculous healing. In prayer, we are able to see God's works of compassion and join with him.

## James's Insight and Instruction

James, the brother of Jesus (an eyewitness of Jesus' life, death and resurrection), says,

> Is anyone among you suffering? Let him pray. Is anyone cheerful? Let him sing praise. Is anyone among you sick? Let him call for the elders of the church, and let them pray over him, anointing him with oil in the name of the Lord. And the prayer of faith will save the one who is sick, and the Lord will raise him up. And if he has committed sins, he will be forgiven. Therefore, confess your sins to one another and pray for one another, that you may be healed. The prayer of a righteous man has great power as it is working. Elijah was a man with a nature like ours, and he prayed fervently that it might not rain, and for three years and six months it did not rain on the earth. Then he prayed again, and heaven gave rain, and the earth bore its fruit. (James 5:13–18)

Prayer for physical or mental healing should always be accompanied by prayer for spiritual healing, including confession of sin. Spiritual healing is at least as important as physical or mental healing. The representatives of the church *and* the sick person need to confess their sins together before praying for healing (v. 16). Mutual confession of sin reminds all present that *all* our righteousness (v. 16) comes to us only from Jesus who forgives *all* our sins.

Most Israelites living in the time of Jesus would not have thought there was any prophet more righteous than Elijah. However, even Elijah who had "a nature like ours" (v. 17) was not completely righteous by the standard of the law, as the record of 1 Kings demonstrates. Thankfully, no one as "righteous" as Elijah has to be present for healing prayers to have a powerful effect. Rather, those who confess their unrighteousness in themselves and cling to Jesus' righteousness can be used by God today in healing prayer.

In prayer for healing, consider anointing with oil in the name of Jesus as a reminder that Jesus and the Holy Spirit are the ones who actualize the healing—not some charismatic person(s) or magical incantation (v. 14). This time of healing prayer can be after a worship service in a quiet place or in the home, which is probably the setting of James. I do not believe it always has to be led by wise elders, though they should provide oversight for all aspects of the church's ministries. Depressed people should consider asking for healing prayer regularly. A friend or family member may need to encourage them to do so.

Understanding the meaning of the Greek word translated as "will raise up" (v. 15) is important. In this context, it clearly indicates an immediate physical rising up. But "raise up" is also the *only* Greek word for resurrection in the New Testament. "Will raise him up" can refer to a present-day, literal standing up in renewed physical or mental health or a future resurrection to complete wholeness (*shalom*) of body, mind, and soul. Whether the sick person is raised up physically or mentally or has to wait until after death, there is power in healing prayer. Because of Jesus' miraculous resurrection, believers who have not been healed physically or mentally in this life will be powerfully resurrected from the dead to wholeness of body, mind, and soul; and they will never become physically or mentally ill again.

The Greek word translated as "save" in verse 15 is also important. It can sometimes refer to being healed physically or mentally, but it usually means salvation from a life of sin in this world or ultimate salvation out of this sinful world through the eventual resurrection of all believers. All three meanings are present in the context of these verses in James.

If a sick person is healed physically or mentally in this life, that person can join those who are cheerfully singing God's praise (v. 13). However, God doesn't expect a false cheerfulness when we are really ill, including illness from clinical depression. Paul's "rejoice in the Lord always" (Philippians 4:4) *always* needs to be balanced with the author of the book of Ecclesiastes's recognition that there is "a time to weep, and a time to laugh" (Ecclesiastes 3:4).

It usually doesn't matter to the healed person whether it is through God's providential healing or through a miraculous healing. The sick person is just glad to be healed. Thankfully, whether healed physically or mentally or not, this person and his/her healers can know that they are *saved* from the grave sickness of sin. The sick person can know for sure that he/she will be completely healed when he/she is *raised up* from the dead. Ultimately every one of us will die, but we need not fear that day as we wait our final, full *salvation*.

Some people think that praying with a particular kind of faith (v. 15) and fervently (v. 17) will always result in prompt physical or mental healing. However, all prayer—not just healing prayer—must be prayed with faith. All prayer must be fervent. But not all our prayers are answered in the way we want. People who are confident of immediate or near-future physical or mental healing as a result of fervent healing prayer should be respected for trying to be faithful to the teaching of this Scripture. We have seen, however, that their belief is based, in part, on a misinterpretation of James 5:13–18. And look at the larger context of this passage in James. Like a farmer who plants seeds and then waits for their growth into "the precious fruit of the earth," James says, "be patient . . . until the coming of the Lord" (v. 7). We may not receive all that we ask for in terms of healing right away. We may have to wait on many aspects of our healing until the second coming of the

Lord. Sadly, a few people may not receive any physical or mental healing at all in this life.

I challenge you to remain steadfast in your love for and commitment to the Lord even if healing is delayed. In fact, remaining steadfast during suffering may actually become a blessing. James says, "Behold, we consider those blessed who remained steadfast" (v. 11). James then goes on to remind his congregation of the steadfastness of Job as an example of someone who waited for a considerable time to be fully restored, including physical healing and healing from depression. What is clearly a curse, like depression, may also very strangely, eventually result in a blessing. Steadfast love for and obedience to Jesus may deepen our relationship with him, which is a great blessing. We may actually come to experience the Lord as "compassionate and merciful" (v. 11), which we may not have experienced when we were depressed.

One caveat to caregivers: don't tell depressed people that their suffering may become a blessing; they won't believe you. It may make them think you are minimizing their suffering, and you may lose their trust. One hopes they will come to the conclusion that their suffering has become a blessing, as well as a curse, on their own several months or several years after their depression resolves.

## Healing Prayer Can Strengthen Our Spiritual Lives

Although healing prayer may not always help us physically or mentally in the way we want in this life, healing prayer nearly always strengthens our spiritual lives. For example, healing prayer may increase our hope in the God who loves us and cares for us, which is often hard to see in the midst of depression. In healing prayer, depressed people are ushered into God's presence, where they may once again get a glimpse of God's compassionate character and the work he has performed on their behalf. As a second example, through prayer we may be empowered by the Holy Spirit to become courageous enough to deal with a long-standing relational conflict contributing to our depression. As a third example, in healing prayer we draw closer to Jesus and depend more on him. Healing prayer enhances our connection with Christ, who is the source of all healing. In fact, many depressed people are more dependent on Jesus than those who are not mentally ill and who consider themselves to be "spiritually healthy." As a final example, in healing prayer we may see a flash of the God of glory who will one day crown the heads of steadfast broken minds with his reflected glory.

Inner healing in healing ministries is a way to help us heal from deep long-standing hurts. Wrong negative views of ourselves may be due, in part, to painful memories. We may have been the victim of some hurtful experience, evil, or injustice. We may have felt distraught and/or justifiably angry at the time we were hurt. However, if these bad memories persist without being dealt with, they often lead to bitterness and resentment, which pollute our minds and hearts and can lead to depression. Again, and again, we become the victim of our own painful memories. Counselors and concerned trained clergy and laypeople can often help with the healing of these painful memories. First, the painful memories need to be uncovered and unhealthy ways of thinking about the memories need to be identified. Then through counsel and prayer with the depressed person, old modes of thinking need to be replaced with new.

One of the most effective ways to overcome these painful memories is to forgive those who have hurt us, as we discussed previously. Christianity as a religion has a lot to say about forgiveness. After all, Jesus forgave his enemies who nailed him to the cross. If he could forgive his torturing enemies, we should forgive those who have hurt us. However, forgiveness is not easy. If we are struggling with unforgiveness, it helps to remember how much God has forgiven us, and we need to plead with Jesus to send the Holy Spirit to cleanse our unforgiving hearts. Addressing deep pain from the past and unforgiveness is often a difficult and prolonged process, but it can be an invaluable way to help depression lift. It also often helps us experience a more intimate relationship with Jesus—sometimes even a closer relationship with those who have hurt us.

> *Dear Lord, thank you for hearing my cries. I am so grateful for this incredible privilege of coming to you in prayer . . . and for how you can use it to bring healing. As I approach your throne of grace, please remind me of your tender compassion and your mighty power. When I earnestly plead for recovery, keep me from thinking that I know better than you—especially if your answer isn't what I want it to be. Enable me to surrender to your will and remain steadfast in my love for you. I know that the benefits and rewards of doing these two things will be very significant.*
>
> *I want to persist in connecting with you through prayer. May this help me to keep my eyes on you—the Source of All Healing. You are able to do the impossible! I want to draw near to you in deep dependence, humility, and trust. Thank you that regardless of the degree of healing experienced in this life, I can know that you will bring complete healing in the next life. Jesus, because you were wounded and broken for us, we will be fully restored and made whole for all eternity! You are amazing!!!*

# 14

## Your Stories: Three Unique Faces of Depression

To HELP YOU SEE how each person's depression is unique but also has common themes with others, I have included the stories of three friends who are kind enough, bold enough, and transparent enough to share their stories. You may identify with some elements of their stories and not with others. Take what helps and leave what doesn't. They will share what the hardest things for them to endure during their depression were and what the most helpful things were. They will also share how depression made their lives different, for better and/or for worse. Remember as you read these stories that most people with depression don't suffer for so long. Fifty percent of people who experience their first depression will never experience another one.

### STUART

Stuart Rupke is seventy years old and is married with two adult children. I have known Stuart since we were both family medicine residents in Charleston, South Carolina, forty-odd years ago. We lived in the same apartment building, and Fenni and I were close friends with Stuart and his wife, Mary. Stu and I almost went into medical practice together. He went to practice family medicine in an underserved area in Virginia and after many years moved to Michigan, where he became faculty in a family medicine residency in Saginaw. He is now retired. We have recently renewed our friendship, which is a great blessing to me. Here is Stuart's story, in his own words.

I have experienced depression off and on since college. I have sometimes thought of it as a mistress with whom I have had a turbulent relationship. I have thought of it also as a weight sitting on me since I sometimes feel a sense of pressure that I cannot lift. For better or for worse, it has been my companion.

It hit me hard when I was a family medicine resident. I was working long hours and feeling exhausted physically and emotionally. I then was assigned to a pediatric oncology unit and had to work with and poke needles into some very sick little ones. I became more and more despondent, thought seriously of suicide, and finally sought help. I fortunately had a very understanding wife and family physician mentor, and was able to get the help I needed. It was not a quick recovery, but it enabled me to continue in my chosen profession.

One of the most difficult aspects of depression for me is a sense of hopelessness. When I am not doing well, the future looks very bleak. I see no end to my despair, despite knowing intellectually that I can get better. I feel like I am in a deep pit with no way out.

Another difficult aspect I have dealt with is a sense of what I can only describe as feeling "dead" inside. This is hard to describe further; to some extent it is almost a lack of emotion. When I feel this way, it is difficult to have empathy for others or to be enthusiastic about anything. The world seems to be colored in shades of gray or black.

A prominent feature of depression for me has been guilt. I frequently review what I have said or should have said to people. I feel guilty for not being a better husband, doctor, friend, citizen. I feel as if I should do more for the people I come in contact with, my patients, my family, and especially the poor and downtrodden. I can't trace this to my parents who were very supportive, but it may partially be due to my Calvinistic beliefs. Most of it seems to be self-generated, however. Guilt can increase a downward spiral until I feel so depressed that I don't care.

Through the years, different things have been helpful to me. The most important has been my faith in Jesus. He has guided and preserved me, even when I don't realize it. Spending time with him in the morning has often been a necessity to make it through the day. Meditating and getting strength from the Psalms has been extremely important. Psalm 139 has really spoken to me over the years. "If I say, 'Surely the darkness shall cover me, and the light about me be night,' even the darkness is not dark to you; the night is bright as the day, for darkness is as light to you" (Psalm 139:11–12). Many other psalms seem to speak about depression, despair, loneliness, and discouragement, and about trusting in God despite these feelings.

Another critical help has been the support I have received from others. My wife has been an incredible support through the years, especially when things look the darkest. Often, she could tell that I was not doing well even before I realized it. My parents were always very supportive and were frequently a helpful presence. Other friends and family have provided an additional network of love and support.

There is no doubt that medication has been very helpful to me over the years. I have at times rebelled against the need to take a pill to feel better, but that is through a false sense of feeling the need to be strong by myself. I have been on various meds and almost all have been helpful. I am thankful for these products of modern medicine.

The concepts behind cognitive therapy have been helpful at times. Recognizing recurrent negative "automatic" thoughts is a starting point. Looking at the evidence for and against a thought is the next step. Then next is posing an alternative thought that makes more sense rationally or based on my core beliefs. This alternative thought may be simply common sense, or it may be based on a verse from Scripture. This approach can help stop a downward spiral or help lift me out of the pit.

A morning routine of exercise, time with the Lord, a shower, and a cup (or more) of coffee have all been helpful to ward off depression. Cultivating thankfulness has been essential.

My life is different because of my experiences with depression. My faith has deepened because of the necessity to look to the Lord for strength. My emotions have been somewhat flattened, partially as a result of medication but perhaps also because of a darker view of life. I still struggle with guilt on most days.

I am very thankful to be in a good place now. On good days, I can even be thankful for my depression or for negative thoughts. As the apostle Paul says, "But by the grace of God I am what I am" (1 Corinthians 15:10). God has been very merciful to me.

Dr. Rupke's experience of recurrent (on and off) depression is illustrative in many ways:

1. He felt helplessness—"a weight . . . a sense of pressure I cannot lift."

2. He was experiencing the stress of a "physically and emotionally" demanding job.

3. Help from family, especially his wife and mentor, was important to him.

4. Hopelessness was "one of the most difficult aspects of depression for me."

5. Stuart experienced painful "lack of emotion"—"feeling dead inside," making it hard to be enthusiastic and have empathy for others.

6. He felt "guilty for not being a better husband, doctor, friend, citizen." Dr. Rupke struggles with guilt most days. I would like to share that I know of no other physician who is kinder to his friends and more empathetic to his patients. I am sure his wife, Mary, would not have asked for a better husband.

7. There were probably some negative effects of religion "due to my Calvinistic beliefs." I am theologically mostly Calvinist in my beliefs, but I am also the first to acknowledge that the modern expression of Calvinism has often been found wanting in its application of the great truths of Scripture to some of the difficulties of living the Christian life—especially some applications of Christian counseling.

8. Religion had been very important to him: "The most important thing has been my faith in Jesus." He spends time daily with God, especially meditating on the Psalms.

9. He found medication to be "very helpful" as one means of common grace through modern medicine.

10. He found cognitive-behavioral therapy to be helpful, including replacing recurrent automatic negative thoughts with evidence-based alternative thoughts. These alternative thoughts can be based on biblically informed common sense or Scripture.

11. He includes exercise in his daily routine.

12. "Cultivating thankfulness has been essential."

13. His faith has deepened because of "the necessity to look to the Lord for strength."

14. He accepts who he is despite his struggles with depression.

# CANDACE

Candace Dodson is fifty-eight years old, married, and has three adult children and one grandson. She has worked in the furniture industry for more than twenty years. I have known Candy as an acquaintance at church for ten years. She regularly decorates the front of our church with flowers that she beautifully arranges. I have been so grateful to become her friend during the past six months as she has attended our depression support group. Here is Candy's story.

I always knew something was "off" with me. It didn't have a name; it wasn't identified. I couldn't express myself in a way that made sense to those around me. I'm not even sure if I tried. There are some very clear and painful memories from my childhood that I can recall—this knowing feeling that I was less than or not fully up to the level of those around me. A sense of shame became how I processed it, that I was a mistake, flawed in some way. As a grade school student, I pulled out my eyelashes—to the point where, I found out years later, they called my mother about it with concern that I was in need of medical attention, which I don't think I ever had. She said it was a phase and I would outgrow it, like someone who bit their nails. And I did. But other compulsive behaviors took its place.

It wasn't until I was in my early thirties that I was officially diagnosed with chronic depression. I had had a classic textbook panic attack (although when it happened, I didn't know that was what it was) in a Walmart; thankfully none of our children were with me that day. I thought I was having a stroke or something. My body had finally sent a signal that I understood and scared me enough to seek medical treatment. Actually, it really scared my husband and my mother, who insisted I see a doctor, because I think I might have ignored it otherwise and found some justifiable reason to shrug it off. That was twenty-five years ago. I have been on antidepressants ever since. I have gone through countless therapists and psychiatrists. I have attended depression classes, clinics, and twelve-step programs.

I was raised in the church, and attended Sunday school, vacation Bible school, was an acolyte, a member of the youth group, but I wasn't really *saved* until I was in my thirties. Because I, like many others, between my early teens and mid-twenties, stopped believing in the church, I sought out and found a family to belong to; it involved drugs, alcohol, two or three attempts at suicide, and worse. But there had been times, one in particular when I was seventeen, when I heard God's voice speak to me.

He was with me, and he got my attention. And then he was gone again, or, more likely, I stopped listening. Around the time I was thirty-five, he came again, and I listened. I renewed my relationship with him and have sought him daily ever since.

When I was told I most likely had been suffering from major depression, anxiety, and compulsive behavior disorders most of my life, I agreed. It was all starting to make sense. There was a name, it had been identified, and I was finally able to express myself and learn I was not the only one. The three hardest things for me when I am experiencing a major depressive episode are not difficult to pinpoint. Although for quite a few years it was kept at bay, at this point in my life I am finding that it creeps back in once or twice a year. Otherwise it stays in remission.

First, I begin to get the racing thoughts, a sense of no control. These prevent me from sleeping well; they distract me from my daily interactions, chores, my professional working duties. The trigger can be and usually is a loved one in distress, a change in my normal daily activity that I didn't orchestrate, and/ or a compulsive behavior showing up after being dormant for a long time. I have described it as an old worn coat that I know is in the closet; all of a sudden, I have somehow managed to put it back on. And for whatever reason, I decide (?) to keep it on and not take it off. Or tell anyone—my husband, close friend, adult children—that the coat is out of the closet.

Second, I slowly shut down emotionally. I can't seem to make decisions about the most ordinary things, like what to wear to work, what to fix for dinner or put on a shopping list for the week. I start to ignore responsibilities like opening mail, paying bills; instead I focus on things that temporarily relieve my stress, like shopping, which is only causes more stress because I am spending, getting lost in a novel (or multiple novels in succession) so I don't have to interact with family members. And I become moody and snappy. I become distracted and am told I don't listen and don't remember things I have been told. It is a spacey kind of oblivion. The worst part is, I know what it is, and I almost like it. I want to sleep, escape, etc.

Last, I come to grips with being in the pit. I know I'm in the pit; I know I let myself get into the pit, and the spiral effect has encompassed all of my being. I get angry, at myself and others. I start dreading each day. I become frozen in feelings and distant with others. My immediate family at this point has figured it out as well, and I would imagine my coworkers too. I demonstrate behavior that is not my normal (healthy) self. It's like the acceptance part of the grieving process. I hate it, and yet I know I must respond and do something to change it. I know I need to use the tools I have in my tool box and get that soft worn coat back into the closet. I have to admit it out loud. To someone. Three of the most helpful things I have learned about myself as a result of my depression also are not difficult to pinpoint. I am not alone. I am loved. God has me in his hands. I know I am not alone because of the countless people I've met or read about who experience this debilitating condition. It is comforting to finally be assured I should not be ashamed, that I am not flawed. I know how much I am loved, as difficult as it still is at times to believe I am worthy of love. I have experienced compassion from others, honest communication from others, and am able to accept this part of my make-up. Last, I know without a doubt that I am a child of God, that he loves me and wants the best for me, and that he is always there for me to turn to, lean on, and depend on during the trials in my life. I just need to show up, because he has always been there, waiting for me.

The result of this journey so far, living with depression, has been both full of sorrow and gratitude. I feel deeply and passionate about many things, people, and conditions. I have empathy and often walk a fine line between wanting to fix things that are wrong and identification of what I should not try to fix. I have learned that no matter how hard it is, at the end of the day, we all have a struggle; it is real, and we often don't see it in others but it is there as well. All we need to do is love—as Jesus loves us. I don't expect much, as my expectations have often left me feeling hopeless, angry, and frustrated. It is not a feeling I enjoy. Without expectations, especially from others, I don't get as disappointed.

Candace's story of recurrent depression is illustrative in many ways:

1. She never remembers a time when she was completely normal. "I always knew something was 'off' with me."

2. She experienced "painful memories from my childhood."

3. She experienced low self-esteem resulting in a "sense of shame."

4. She had compulsive behaviors like pulling out her eyelashes.

5. Panic attacks accompanied her chronic depression, and they were what led her to seek medical treatment.

6. She has been on antidepressants since the age of thirty and they helped.

7. She has participated in many individual and group counseling sessions.

8. She was attracted to the wrong crowd that involved drugs, alcohol, and "worse" when she was young.

9. She has had suicide attempts.

10. Her relationship with God was renewed when she was about thirty-five.

11. She found a diagnosis of "major depression, anxiety, and compulsive behavior disorder" helpful in making sense of her symptoms. In a day when "labeling" is so frowned upon in mental healthcare, Candace shows that making a diagnosis can often be helpful.

12. At times she has the presence of some bipolar symptoms like racing thoughts, sleeplessness, easy distractibility, and poor functioning in activities at home and at work.

13. A variety of things can trigger a depression.

14. She finds it difficult "to make decisions about the most ordinary things."

15. She fails to meet responsibilities.

16. She withdraws from people to avoid interaction.

17. She gets irritable and angry.

18. She has trouble concentrating and is easily distracted.

19. She becomes "frozen in feelings and distant with others."

20. Her behavior is not her normal healthy self.

21. She recognizes that she needs to be a part of her recovery.

22. She finds sharing her pain with others to be helpful.

23. She knows that she is not alone, that she is loved by God. "I know without a doubt that I am a child of God."

24. She is helped by knowing that others have experienced what she has experienced, and this helps her to not feel ashamed.

25. She is helped by compassion and honest communication from others.

26. She has come to accept that depression is a part of who she is.

27. She knows that God "wants the best for me."

28. She can "depend on [God] during the trials of my life."

29. Depression has helped her feel more deeply and passionately about many things.

30. She is more empathetic but also recognizes there is only so much you can do for others.

31. She does not expect too much from other people.


## BRENDA

Brenda is sixty-eight years old, married, and has an adopted adult son and daughter-in-law. Brenda works in website and e-communication support for a small nonprofit organization. She has a beautiful voice, which she uses in church. I value her friendship, which started when she attended a mini-series on depression that I led almost a year ago. Here is Brenda's story.

> I have had three periods of depression. All three involved disappointments, along with a spiritual component, given my faith in God. I found relief through the help of counselors, friends, and increasing sense of connection with God. During the second of the three periods, I also found relief through medication.
>
> I slid into the first of the three episodes through naivete concerning general difficulties of life and my lack of sainthood. I agreed wholeheartedly with M. Scott Peck's opening line of his best seller *The Road Less Traveled: A New Psychology of Love, Traditional Values and Spiritual Growth*: "Life is difficult." As a Christian, this "difficult life" took me by surprise, and I was utterly disappointed.
>
> Three things rescued me from despair:
>
> My husband remained committed to me (and our relationship).
>
> Together we went to a counselor who helped us recalibrate our expectations, set goals, and discover ways to build our relationship. (For example, a simple behavioral change was to establish a *planned weekly time* to talk about ourselves.)
>
> I had a significant dream that ended with a clear, personal message from God that put everything in perspective. It renewed my trust in God and gave me hope.
>
> My second struggle with depression occurred about ten years later, after a few years of seeking medical help for infertility. As we gave up the treatment process, my resentment grew toward those who easily became pregnant. I became intensely angry at God, who I believed could do something about it. Knowing there was no future in battling God, I found a therapist who could help me sort out my faith and cope with the disappointment. (She unexpectedly helped me consider adoption

as an option to starting a family.) I also started taking an antidepressant, which brought quick relief to the dark heaviness of depression. When it took effect, I felt as if I had taken off a leaded vest, or as if dark clouds dissipated to reveal a clear day.

I continued taking Zoloft for about twelve years. Then, wondering if I still needed it, I cut back to a low dosage (half of what I had been taking) for another two years. By that point, I had made a few changes in lifestyle—exercising more and connecting with God and friends in more substantive ways. I stopped taking the antidepressant altogether. Through a series of classes and spiritual disciplines, I enjoyed a more positive approach to daily life.

However, my third experience with depression came in 2018, after a year of unbearably stressful changes and losses: retirement, moving out of our family home to another part of the state, preparing for our son's wedding, and caring for my mother in a nursing home 800 miles away—these were almost more than I could bear. In a three-week period, it was all over. We moved, my mother passed away, and our son and daughter-in-law were married—leaving me to grieve for the next year. My husband and friends gently suggested I consider taking an antidepressant again. But for me, at that particular time, I felt my grief was necessary, that I had the tools to manage it, and that over time it would subside. I joined a grief support group and continued finding comfort in spiritual disciplines.

My depression did subside, and then it ended abruptly after a prayer session at an Immanuel Approach Healing Prayer conference (led by Dr. Karl Lehman). Much like the dream in my first period of depression, I had an encounter with God that put everything in perspective. This time he convinced me of his deeply personal love for me.

Joy is being with people who are glad to be with us. I've come to realize that at the top of that list is God, whose face lights up when I come to him. Depression, on the other hand, is an isolating condition. We cannot believe anyone wants to be with us. We don't want to be with ourselves.

I believe we were made to be relational. My relief from depression came partly with the help of medication, but mostly by way of relationships (counselors, family, and a support group) and turning toward (not away from) God.

Brenda's story of recurrent depression is illustrative in many ways:

1. Disappointments triggered all three depressions.

2. There was a spiritual component in all three.

3. Counselors, friends, and connection with God helped in all three.

4. During one depression, medication helped.

5. The difficulties of life caught her off guard because she was naïve about them and did not have enough maturity in her faith to deal with them. (By the way, there is nothing wrong with lacking maturity in faith—it takes time even in the best of circumstances.)

6. Her husband's commitment to her was essential.

7. She worked with her husband on their relationship.

8. God spoke to her through a dream that renewed her trust in God.

9. Infertility fueled resentment towards other and anger toward God.

10. A Christian psychologist helped her get a new perspective on her faith and helped her with coping skills.

11. After twelve years on an antidepressant, she felt she no longer needed it.

12. Exercise was a help.

13. Spiritual disciplines helped.

14. Her third depression was triggered by the coalescence of multiple stressors: retirement, a move, preparing for her son's wedding, and caring for a frail mother who died.

15. Healthy grieving helped with her losses.

16. God revealed his deeply personal love for her during a session of prayer.

17. Being with others who enjoy being with her brings her joy.

18. Medications helped but relationships with God and others (including counselors, families, and support groups) were the most helpful.

# Conclusion

I HAVE TRIED TO be completely transparent in sharing my story of depression with you. So have Stuart, Candace, and Brenda. Even Job and the weeping prophet Jeremiah have shared their stories with you. Now I hope you can share your story of depression with someone you trust, such as (1) a physician (especially a psychiatrist or a primary care physician) or other healthcare professional or (2) a counselor or clergyperson, or (3) a family member or trusted friend. You may feel a little bit better just by sharing your story, and those you share it with may be able to help you with your depression or direct you to the right person.

Your experience of depression is, in part, unique to you. But you also have depressive features in common with other depressed people. If you think you might be depressed, score yourself on a PHQ-9 form on page 33 and 34. If you score in the depressed range, consider talking with a healthcare provider or counselor. If you are thinking about suicide, you must talk with someone right away. If there is no one else to turn to, call and talk with someone at the National Suicide Prevention Lifeline: 800–273-8255.

If you know someone who you think may be depressed, consider asking two questions: Do you have little interest or pleasure in doing things? Have you been feeling down, depressed, or hopeless? If this person answers yes to either question, gently encourage getting help. Also prayerfully consider if Jesus wants you to come alongside this needy person as a loyal, loving presence. This is no small task.

As you now know, there are biomedical and psychosocial aspects of depression. If you are frightened by medications (I think needlessly frightened), consider seeking help from a counselor. If you find counseling too unsettling right now, consider medication. If you are willing, my recommendation is to get help from both a healthcare professional and a counselor, especially if you are moderately depressed or worse.

Many medications are well known to be effective in treating depression. Antidepressants do not make you feel like a different person. Most will begin to feel like their old selves. And serious side effects are rare. If unpleasant side effects are too bothersome, you can be switched to an antidepressant that does not have the same side effect profile. Many of these medications are very inexpensive.

Counseling for depression is also well known to be effective in treating depression. Psychoeducation and talk therapy are important to all depressed people. Cognitive-behavioral therapy (CBT) and interpersonal therapy (IPT) are two of the most research-supported counseling approaches for depression. Neither approach is inconsistent with living out your Christian faith, and both will likely help heal you from depression. Consider CBT if you have a pessimistic outlook on life and/or have automatic negative thoughts (ANTs). Consider IPT if your depression has adversely affected important relationships in your life and/or if one or more of your relationships contribute(s) to your depression. Many other counseling approaches may be helpful to you, but they have less scientific evidence for their effectiveness.

In addition to the biomedical and psychosocial aspects of depression, the spiritual aspects need to be addressed for complete healing. If there are things that you believe about God and/or the church that seem to negatively affect you, consider talking with your clergyperson or even a friend who is a committed knowledgeable lay Christian. He/she may be able to help you sort out what are spiritual truths from what are spiritual myths. If there are spiritual disciplines that help you with your depression, practice them even more. If you think you need more spiritual help reread chapters 12 and 13 and talk with one of those just mentioned. He or she may have ideas that you never thought of and may be a source encouragement as you take advantage of spiritual helps.

I may not know you personally, but I really do care about anyone reading this book. Almost daily, I bring you in prayer into the presence of God. For more personal prayer, seek out a Christian who believes in healing prayer. That may be a clergyperson or a committed lay Christian. If God does not choose to heal you in the way you have prayed for, try to endure your suffering by waiting with hope. Regardless of how you feel, regularly remind yourself that you are in the hands of Jesus and you are the apple of your Father's eye. The Holy Spirit within you will bring about the healing that God has planned for you, which may be only healing in part in this life, but, thankfully, will be complete in the next. Rarely, there will be no healing from depression in this life. If you are one of them and still trust in Jesus your life is an incredible witness to me of your steadfast love for your Father.

Writing this book has been a labor of love, but it has been a slow process. Untangling a life that has experienced seven depressions takes time. It also takes time to sort out what is true and helpful from what is not true and is unhelpful in the biomedical, psychosocial, and Christian spiritual literature. As you close this book, I would like to leave you with what I think are the two most important things I have learned in this writing process. First, God in Jesus Christ is truly faithful. In my darkest days and blackest nights, he has been trustworthy—he is someone I can hope in. I try to spend time with him every day. Second, loving and being loved by my family, friends, and the many people who Christ calls my neighbors has been a lifeline. I am now devoting much more of my time and energy to nurturing those relationships, especially with those suffering from depression.

# APPENDIX A

*Drug Treatments for Depression*

## DRUG TREATMENTS FOR UNIPOLAR DEPRESSION

### SSRIs and Their Ilk

I AM INDEBTED TO *Clinical Psychopharmacology* (see Selective Bibliography) for much of the information in this Appendix. First, we will look at selective serotonin reuptake inhibitors (SSRIs), including their side effects, in some detail, because some patients resist considering antidepressant medications and some counselors discourage their use because of side effects. You will see how minor most of the side effects are. And most people do not experience any side effects.

To follow is a table that shows the currently available SSRIs in the United States. Generic medications are written without capital letters, and brand-name medications are capitalized. Generic medications are usually less expensive (sometimes much less expensive) than brand-name medications and almost always work just as well.

| Generic | Brand Name |
|---------|-----------|
| citalopram | Celexa |
| escitalopram | Lexapro |
| fluoxetine | Prozac |
| fluvoxamine | Luvox (this brand is not available in the US) |
| paroxetine | Paxil |
| sertraline | Zoloft |

SSRIs are the most commonly prescribed antidepressants, for a number of reasons:

First, SSRIs are very effective. There is a 50 to 70 percent chance of complete remission or significant improvement from depression with the first SSRI prescribed in your first depression. However, it usually takes two to four weeks for improvement to begin and four to eight weeks for the medication to take full effect. Doses may need to be increased if there is insufficient improvement at the end of four to eight weeks. When maximal improvement has been reached, the drug must be continued for another six to nine months to prevent relapse. The medication should often be continued for life if the current depression is the second episode of major depression. And the medication should almost always be continued for life if the current episode is the third episode or more of major depression. The medication may be continued for life if the first depression is particularly severe or prolonged. The goal in treating depression should always be to get the patient back to normal, not just better. This can't always be accomplished, but there are many different rational adjustments in medications that can move a patient from better to normal, sometimes better than normal if he/she has dysthymia (persistent depressive disorder).

Second, SSRIs are affordable. As we have said, SSRIs now come in inexpensive generic forms, which are almost always just as effective as many newer brand-name SSRIs.

Third, SSRIs are not addicting. There is no craving for the medication. SSRIs (especially paroxetine/Paxil) should, however, be gradually reduced when they are discontinued to prevent discontinuation symptoms such as anxiety, insomnia, headache, dizziness, fatigue, irritability, nausea, electric shock-like symptoms, and flulike symptoms. Of course, the patient needs to be on the alert for symptoms of recurring depression. If the depression recurs, it should be treated again with the same antidepressant, possibly for life. However, taking an SSRI does not make it more likely that you will need it for life.

Fourth, there are just a few common side effects of SSRIs, which only a minority of patients experience.

1. On initiation of treatment there may be nausea and diarrhea, which usually resolves in one to two weeks.

2. Initially there may also be anxiety, restlessness, and insomnia that usually resolves in one to two weeks. In fact, as the antidepressants take effect, there usually is a reduction in these symptoms.

Benzodiazepine Use in Depression: *If the anxiety and/or restlessness is severe enough (whether caused by the depression or as a temporary side effect of an antidepressant) your doctor may prescribe a short-term course of a tranquilizer, specifically a benzodiazepine such as diazepam (Valium), alprazolam (Xanax), lorazepam (Ativan), or clonazepam (Klonopin). Benzodiazepines work immediately for almost everyone, but are usually used for only a short period of time at the beginning of treatment, as they can cause dependence or even addiction with long-term use. They have to be very carefully prescribed, or not prescribed at all, in patients with a history of substance use disorder. I have not experienced problems weaning people off benzodiazepines when used for significant anxiety due to the depression or an early antidepressant side effect as long as I make sure the patient understands when starting the benzodiazepine that it is not a long-term solution to the anxiety. Counseling is also often helpful for symptoms of anxiety. Common side effects of benzodiazepines, especially in the elderly, are over-sedation, disequilibrium, and memory loss or falls, so they need to be started in small doses. Benzodiazepine should be prescribed in small amounts to depressed patients with suicidal thoughts since an overdose, especially if combined with alcohol, can be fatal.*

Another medication for anxiety that is not addictive is buspirone (Buspar), but it takes several weeks to become effective; it also has mild antidepressant effects. If the insomnia is severe enough, the healthcare professional may prescribe a sleeping pill. Especially good for insomnia is trazodone (Oleptro) and mirtazapine (Remeron), as they are not addictive and also have antidepressant properties. Short-term use of a benzodiazepine may be indicated if trazodone or mirtazapine are ineffective.

3. Sexual dysfunction is a common late side effect of SSRIs. When sexual dysfunction occurs, it does not usually resolve until the SSRI is decreased or discontinued. Decreased libido and anorgasmia (or delayed orgasm) in both men and women and erectile dysfunction in men

are the three most common sexual side effects. Often there is sexual dysfunction from the depression itself, which improves as the depression improves. Not infrequently patients with sexual side effects feel so much better, in terms of depression, that they decide to live with the sexual dysfunction. There are ways to enjoy physical intimacy apart from sexual intercourse. Viagra and two related drugs, Cialis and Levitra, often help both men and women with sexual dysfunction.

4. Weight gain, from eating more due to an increase in appetite, may develop later in the course of SSRI treatment. It can be prevented by restricting caloric intake and engaging in regular exercise. However, many depressed people have a hard time getting motivated to eat right and exercise. Even five minutes of exercise a day is a good start.

5. Apathy with decreased spontaneity and decreased sense of emotional aliveness is an occasional late side effect. Again, some people feel so much better in terms of other depressive symptoms that they are willing to put up with this side effect. Apathy can also be a symptom of depression itself and may actually improve with an SSRI.

6. SSRIs can precipitate manic, mixed manic and depression, or hypomanic symptoms in people with bipolar disorder. Mood stabilizers alone or sometimes in combination with SSRIs are necessary in bipolar depression to prevent or treat mania, mixed mania and depression, and hypomania. Mood stabilizers themselves often help bipolar depression. Antidepressants alone should never be the treatment for bipolar disorder.

7. The most serious side effect of SSRIs is serotonin syndrome. It is rare and is almost always due to (a) very excessive doses of a medication with serotonin effects or (b) the combination of multiple medications and/or other compounds like St. John's wort with each adding to the serotonin effects. The symptoms of serotonin syndrome include confusion, agitation, loss of muscle coordination, and excessive sweating. The symptoms of serotonin syndrome are rare; even more rarely, they can be fatal. My psychiatrist once told me he had never seen a clear-cut case of serotonin syndrome except from intentional drug overdose. A neurologist friend of mine told me the same thing.

There are two new antidepressants that partially inhibit the reuptake of serotonin (like SSRIs) but also have a direct action at serotonin receptor sites. They are vilazodone (Viibryd) and vortioxetine (Trintellix). We are only beginning to figure out in what circumstances they best fit into the treatment of depression. They seem to be especially effective on improving concentration. Needless to say, they are very expensive because they are new.

One alternative medicine plant substance, St. John's wort, has serotonin activity and has many positive effects on depression. It is in many over-the-counter products for depression. These products vary greatly in their potency, making it hard to know how much of the active substance is in the varying formulations. Treatment starts at 300 mg per day and may be increased to as high as 1800 mg per day. St. John's wort should not be combined with antidepressants that have serotonin activity. Because St. John's wort is not regulated by the Federal Drug Administration many healthcare professionals, myself included, do not recommend it. I would strongly advise against using it in moderately severe and severe depression, because its effectiveness in treatment with this level of severity has not been proven. Your healthcare professional, however, would definitely want to know if you are taking St. John's wort.

## SNRIs

Another class of antidepressant medication is the serotonin-norepinephrine reuptake inhibitors (SNRIs). Like SSRIs, they partially inhibit the reuptake of serotonin, but they also partially inhibit the reuptake of norepinephrine.

Below is a table that shows the currently available SNRIs. If you are on an SNRI, you should find your medication here.

| Generic | Brand Name |
| --- | --- |
| desvenlafaxine | Pristiq |
| duloxetine | Cymbalta |
| levomilnacipran | Fetzima |
| milnacipran | Savella |
| venlafaxine | Effexor |

Overall, SNRIs are as effective as SSRIs. But sometimes an SNRI works when a SSRI doesn't and sometimes vice versa. SNRIs can cause the same serotonin induced side effects as SSRIs, as well as some norepinephrine-induced side effects such as palpitations, high blood pressure, excessive sweating, increased anxiety, restlessness, and insomnia. Fortunately, the anxiety, restlessness, and insomnia often resolve with continued use as the depression improves. Benzodiazepine tranquilizers for anxiety and restlessness and trazodone and mirtazapine for insomnia are as effective as with SSRIs. Serious side effects are rare. SNRIs may need to be reduced or discontinued if the side effects are severe enough. Five percent of patients will develop very high blood pressures, so blood-pressure testing needs to be done shortly after starting an SNRI. SNRIs may be especially helpful when apathy, low energy, pervasive loss of interest, and low motivation are prominent symptoms. Unfortunately, SNRIs are somewhat more expensive than many SSRIs. The cheapest are generic duloxetine and venlafaxine. Venlafaxine is more likely than other SNRIs to cause discontinuation symptoms so should be withdrawn slowly.

## Bupropion

Bupropion (Wellbutrin) is the only antidepressant that partially inhibits the reuptake of both norepinephrine and dopamine. Common side effects of bupropion are nausea, constipation, dizziness, dry mouth, weight loss, anxiety, restlessness, and insomnia. In my experience, the anxiety, restlessness, and insomnia are worse with bupropion than either SSRIs or SNRIs. I almost always prescribe a benzodiazepine tranquilizer for a short time for anxiety and restlessness and trazodone or mirtazapine for insomnia if these side effects are pronounced on initiation of bupropion. Bupropion has no sexual side effects, which is very important to some depressed people. Serious side effects are rare, but it should not be prescribed to people with a seizure disorder, because it can trigger a seizure. It does not cause seizures in people who do not have a seizure disorder. It should also not be prescribed for people with anorexia or bulimia. Like SNRIs, bupropion (Wellbutrin) may be especially helpful when apathy, low energy, pervasive loss of interest, and low motivation are prominent symptoms.

## Reuptake Summary

I estimate that 80 to 90 percent of the antidepressants I prescribe act by reducing the reuptake of one or more of the neurotransmitters serotonin, norepinephrine, and dopamine. SSRIs, SNRIs, and bupropion all act by increasing our own neurotransmitters in synapses; they thereby stimulate more receptors on the receiving neuron. It is not surprising, then, that these medications are so safe and effective in the treatment of depression. These medications, however, are not happy pills. In people who do not have depression, they have no effect at all.

## Mirtazapine

Mirtazapine (Remeron) is an antidepressant that is in a class by itself and its mechanism of action is unknown. It often causes sedation, so it may not be the best drug when there is already very low energy. On the other hand, it may be the ideal drug when there is insomnia. It also causes an increased appetite with weight gain, so it may not be the best drug when the patient is already troubled by obesity. However, it may be the ideal drug when there is unwanted weight loss. Mirtazapine has no clinically significant effect on sexual function. It is also often used to potentiate other antidepressants and has some effect on anxiety.

## Trazodone

Trazodone is another antidepressant in a class by itself, and its mechanism of action is unknown. It is not as effective as other antidepressants, but it is often used to potentiate other antidepressants. It is sedating, so it is especially helpful when insomnia is present due to the depression or as a side effect from the primary antidepressant used.

## Buspirone

Buspirone (Buspar) has mild antidepressant and antianxiety properties and is in a class by itself. In my experience, it does not work at all in about half of patients. But it sometimes helps augment the antidepressant effects of SSRIs. It also rarely has significant side effects.

## Tricyclic Antidepressants

Tricyclic antidepressants (TCAs) are used less frequently today due to their side effects. There are, however, times when they are used, especially in treatment-resistant depression. The tricyclic antidepressants have an effect on the serotonin and/or norepinephrine receptors. In addition, they often cause significant sedation and side effects, such a dry mouth, constipation, difficulty urinating, blurry vision, and a sudden drop in blood pressure upon standing, which can cause fainting. In geriatric patients, they can cause confusion. Particularly problematic is the fact that less than a one-month supply of a tricyclic antidepressant is often enough to be lethal in a suicidal overdose. Small doses of amitriptyline or nortriptyline may be helpful in depressed patients with insomnia.

Below is a table that shows the tricyclic antidepressants currently available.

| Generic | Brand |
|---------|-------|
| imipramine | Tofranil |
| desipramine | Norpramin |
| amitriptyline | Elavil |
| nortriptyline | Pamelor |
| doxepin | Sinequan |

## Monoamine Oxidase Inhibitors

Monoamine oxidase inhibitors (MAOIs) are used even less frequently than tricyclic antidepressants because they require significant dietary and medication restrictions, which if not followed can cause serious, even fatal, side effects.

## Ketamine

Ketamine has been available in an intravenous formulation for anesthesia for many years. It now comes with an intranasal delivery system (esketamine = Spravato), which has just been approved by the Federal Drug Administration. It is starting to be used in moderate to severe major depression in those who have failed at least three other antidepressant treatments (so-called treatment-resistant depression). It works almost immediately and lasts for two to six weeks, at which time it can be repeated if necessary. It can be repeated indefinitely. Its side effects include dizziness, high blood pressure, confusion, and feeling of detachment from reality, which can be frightening. Either dosage formulation needs to be given with monitoring in the office or clinic for two hours. Little is known about the long-term side effects of this drug. However, many experts think ketamine is a major breakthrough in the treatment of major depression.

## Combining Antidepressants

When an antidepressant only partially relieves a depression, a second antidepressant may be added. Common combinations are a SSRI or a SNRI with bupropion, mirtazapine or trazodone. Bupropion may be especially effective if there is apathy, low energy, pervasive loss of interest, and low motivation because of its activating effect. It may not be a good choice if anxiety is a prominent symptom. Mirtazapine is especially helpful when there is significant insomnia and a decreased appetite. In a patient struggling with obesity it may not be the best choice. Trazodone is especially helpful if there is insomnia. It has only mild antidepressant properties but sometimes it is enough to put a partially treated depression into complete remission.

## Augmenting Antidepressants

Another approach when an antidepressant is only partially effective is to augment with another agent. Lithium or an atypical antipsychotic are commonly used (see below). Also, a thyroid medicine called liothyronine (Cytomel) and the stimulant methylphenidate (Ritalin) are sometimes useful in augmenting an antidepressant. Cytomel or Ritalin are not commonly used but may be helpful when there is apathy, low energy, pervasive loss of interest, and low motivation. I find Ritalin to be especially helpful in seniors with these symptoms.

## BIPOLAR TREATMENTS

Lithium is a mood stabilizer that has been around for many years. It is safe, effective, and inexpensive. It also works fairly quickly, in several days to a week or two. Because it can cause serious side effects at too high a dose, blood levels need to be periodically monitored. Common side effects include nausea, tremulousness, and increased thirst and urination. More serious side effects such as kidney damage (rare) or low thyroid hormone (fairly common), require periodic monitoring with blood and urine tests. If lithium causes kidney damage, it must be stopped; if it causes low thyroid hormone, the deficiency can easily be replaced with safe thyroid hormone medications.

Atypical antipsychotic mood stabilizers are very effective and work quickly, in several days to a week or two. However, they often have more problematic side effects. Sometimes there are neurologic side effects. These neurologic side effects are much less frequent with atypical antipsychotics than typical ones. Parkinson's disease-like side symptoms, including tremor and motor restlessness, can occur early in treatment, but are usually mild and are quickly reversible. Uncommonly bizarre, involuntary movements, especially of the tongue and face, called tardive dyskinesia, can occur after long-term use and is not always reversible. Because of the risk of tardive dyskinesia, monitoring for early signs of it is important. Less serious side effects, such as sedation, dry mouth, blurred vision, difficulty urinating and low blood pressure, can occur early in treatment. If these symptoms are mild, the medication can be continued, because the symptoms will often improve or even resolve after one or two weeks. One of the most troubling side effects is weight gain, especially the kind that can lead to metabolic syndrome and/or diabetes. Because the antipsychotics are so quickly effective, they are sometimes used short-term until other mood stabilizers with slower onset of action take effect. Sometimes small doses of these medications are effective. Olanzapine (Zyprexa), quetiapine (Seroquel) and aripiprazole (Abilify) are among the older atypical antipsychotic that are relatively inexpensive, while lurasidone (Latuda) and paliperidone (Invega) are newer and more expensive (often very expensive). There are many other atypical antipsychotics that cost somewhere in between.

The antiseizure mood stabilizer lamotrigine (Lamictal) is safe, effective, and inexpensive. It has few side effects, but one can be serious, namely a severe rash. The rash can be prevented by starting with low doses and slowly increasing the dose. This, however, results in a delay in effectiveness for six to eight weeks. Atypical antipsychotic medications may be used simultaneously until lamotrigine becomes effective.

The antiseizure mood stabilizer divalproex (Depakote) is inexpensive and often effective in one or two weeks. It can cause serious side effects at doses that are too high, so blood levels must be periodically monitored. Rarely the liver can be affected even at low doses, so blood liver function tests may be frequently checked during the first six months of treatment. Divalproex can cause serious birth defects, so it should never be used in women of child-bearing age.

The antiseizure mood stabilizer carbamazepine (Tegretol) is more effective than Depakote and inexpensive, but it is difficult to determine the proper dosage, needs blood levels monitored, and has two rare but serious side effects: a dangerously low blood cell count and serious skin rashes.

# Appendix B

## Brief Screening Tools for Depression, Suicide, Bipolar Disorder, and Anxiety

### DEPRESSION

1. Do you have little interest or pleasure in doing things?
2. Have you been feeling down, depressed, or hopeless?

### SUICIDE

1. Have you recently had thoughts of killing yourself?
2. Are you considering killing yourself now?

### BIPOLAR DISORDER

1. Have you ever had periods of increased energy?
2. Have you ever had periods of decreased need for sleep?

## ANXIETY

1.  Do you feel nervous, anxious, or on edge?
2.  Are you not able to stop or control your worry?

# Appendix C

## God's Promises to Remember When You Are Depressed

"For all the promises of God find their Yes in him [Jesus]."

2 Corinthians 1:20

*When you are lonely or feel abandoned:*

Moses says to Joshua on the verge of taking possession of the promised land: "It is the Lord who goes before you. He will be with you; he will not leave you or forsake you. Do not fear or be dismayed" (Deuteronomy 31:8).

The prophet Isaiah says of the Lord regarding his redeemed people: "When you pass through the waters, I will be with you; and through the rivers, they shall not overwhelm you; when you walk through fire you shall not be burned, and the flame shall not consume you" (Isaiah 43:2).

The very last thing Jesus said on earth before his ascension to heaven: "I am with you always, to the end of the age" (Matthew 28:20).

The author of the book of Hebrews reminds the young persecuted church that God had said: "I will never leave you nor forsake you" (Hebrews 13:5).

Paul says of those justified through Christ Jesus's death and resurrection: "Who shall separate us from the love of Christ? Shall tribulation, or distress, or persecution, or famine, or nakedness, or danger, or sword? . . . I am sure that neither death nor life, nor angels nor rulers, nor things present nor things to come, nor powers, nor height nor depth, nor anything else in all creation, will be able to separate us from the love of God in Christ Jesus our Lord" (Romans 8:35, 38–39).

## When you think you are a failure or feel worthless:

You are "the apple of his [God's] eye" (Deuteronomy 32:10) and "he who touches you touches the apple of his [God's] eye" (Zechariah 2:8), the most sensitive spot in the human body.

King David in Psalm 139:13–14 says: "You formed my inward most parts; you knitted me together in my mother's womb. I praise you, for I am fearfully and wonderfully made. Wonderful are your works."

In Psalm 8:3–5, David says, "When I look at your heavens, the work of your fingers, the moon and the stars, which you have set in place, what is man that you are mindful of him, and the son of man that you care for him? Yet you have made him a little lower than the heavenly beings and crowned him with glory and honor."

The Apostle Paul in Ephesians 2:10 says to those who have been saved by faith because of grace, "We are his workmanship, created in Christ Jesus for good works."

## When you feel anxious or fearful:

When we are anxious, we should do what Peter says the flock of God should be doing, that is, "casting all your anxieties on him [Jesus the chief shepherd], because he cares for you" (1 Peter 5:7).

The psalmist reminds us: "When the cares of my heart are many, your [the Lord's] consolations cheer my soul" (Psalm 94:19).

Paul encourages those who are anxious to share their anxiety with God through prayer and then says: "And the peace of God, which surpasses all understanding, will guard your hearts and your minds in Christ Jesus" (Philippians 4:7).

Jesus knew that his disciples would be fearful when they faced threatening situations. Jesus encouraged them that even after he left them physically: "In me you may have peace. In the world you will have tribulation. But take heart; I have overcome the world" (John 16:33).

*When you feel broken and weak:*

King David says of the righteous [those who try to completely trust and obey the Lord], "The Lord is near to the brokenhearted and saves the crushed in spirit" (Psalm 34:18).

King David says of God regarding the outcasts and afflicted: "He heals the brokenhearted, and binds up their wounds" (Psalm 147:3).

Isaiah prophesied regarding the coming Messiah: "He has sent me to bind up the brokenhearted . . . to comfort all who mourn; to grant those who mourn in Zion—to give them a beautiful headdress instead of ashes, the oil of gladness instead of mourning, the garment of praise instead of a faint spirit" (Isaiah 61:1–3).

In 2 Corinthians 12:9–10, the Lord says to Paul: "My grace is sufficient for you, for my power is made perfect in weakness," and Paul notes in response, "I am content with weaknesses . . . For when I am weak, then I am strong."

*When you wonder whether there is any meaning in your suffering:*

The Apostle Paul says: "Suffering produces endurance, and endurance produces character, and character produces hope" (Romans 5:3–4).

Jesus' brother James says: "The testing of your faith produces steadfastness. And let steadfastness have its full effect, that you may be perfect and complete" (James 1:2–3).

In 2 Corinthians 1:4, Paul says the God of all comfort "comforts us in all our affliction, so that we may be able to comfort those who are in any affliction, with the comfort with which we ourselves are comforted by God."

*When you need healing prayer:*

Jeremiah prays: "Heal me, O Lord, and I shall be healed; save me and I shall be saved, for you are my praise" (Jeremiah 17:14).

As Jesus inaugurated the kingdom of heaven, he healed many: "And Jesus went throughout all the cities and villages, teaching in the synagogues and proclaiming the gospel of the kingdom and healing every disease and every affliction" (Matthew 9:35). The healing kingdom of heaven was breaking into the broken kingdom of this world.

*Waiting with hope:*

Isaiah brings hope to those who feel as if the Lord is not watching over them: "Have you not known? Have you not heard? The Lord is the everlasting God, the Creator of the ends of the earth. He does not faint or grow weary; his understanding is unsearchable. He gives power to the faint, and to him who has no might he increases strength. Even youths shall faint and be weary, and young men shall fall exhausted; but they who wait for the Lord shall renew their strength; they shall mount up like eagles; they shall run and not be weary; they shall walk and not faint" (Isaiah 40:28–31).

Jeremiah says: "But this I call to mind, and therefore I have hope: The steadfast love of the Lord never ceases; his mercies never come to an end; they are new every morning; great is your faithfulness. 'The Lord is my portion,' says my soul, 'therefore I will hope in him'" (Lamentations 3:21–24).

In the new heaven and new earth when God makes his dwelling place with humanity, as Jesus did when he was on earth: "He will wipe away every tear from their eyes, and death shall be no more, neither shall there be mourning, nor crying, nor pain anymore, for the former things have passed away" (Revelation 21:4).

Paul says: "The sufferings of this present time are not worth comparing with the glory that is to be revealed to us" (Romans 8:18).

# Appendix D

## *Praying with Laurelle Moody*

The following are fourteen prayers that you previously found after relevant sections of this book. I met Laurelle Moody when she was about four years old, riding her rocking horse in the home of my now close friend of forty years, Pastor Jeff Moody. For years, Laurelle has experienced the physical and mental suffering of chronic Lyme disease. She has recently started to improve and is willing to share the kinds of prayers that helped sustain her. You may want to pray a different prayer every morning on a biweekly cycle.

*When you are lonely or feel abandoned:*

My Lord, who sticks closer than a brother, I feel so lonely! It seems like you have abandoned me in this place of barren emptiness. I cry out to you and hear no reply. It feels like no one knows or understands me or my pain. Yet I realize, Jesus, that you know and understand. You were a man of sorrows who experienced utter abandonment—total aloneness. Though I feel hollow inside, I know that your Holy Spirit lives within me. Please help me to believe that you never leave or forsake me.

I ask you to give me wisdom to make good choices so that I don't isolate myself from the very people you are calling to walk with me and provide uplifting support. When I know I should connect with others but don't have it in me to take the necessary steps, please become my motivation and inspiration.

Thank you for making me part of your family. You created us to need each other. Still, I know relationships can be hard. Let me find comfort in knowing that when others fail me or I fail others, you are always faithful. Thank you for being my constant companion.

## *When you feel as if you are a failure or worthless:*

My Creator, who formed me with infinite wisdom and tender care, it is hard to come to you right now. It seems like everything I do falls short, and I don't measure up . . . My weaknesses, flaws, and inabilities make me feel like such a failure! Between my shortcomings and my sins, I imagine that you shake your head in disgust. Yet your Word says that isn't true. Even when I fail, you run to embrace me whenever I turn to you! Jesus, thank you for dying on the cross and securing my forgiveness. You must treasure me more than I can comprehend to pay such a high price!

Still, I wrestle with a deep sense of worthlessness. Please remind me that my worth is not wrapped up in my performance. It is so easy to rely on my own negative thoughts, feelings, and evaluations when defining myself. But you say that I am a whole new creation in Christ Jesus—designed to do good works! Strengthen my faith. Help me believe that you can take my imperfect offerings and use them in meaningful ways. Thank you for redeeming my failures and investing so much to prove how deeply you value me.

## *When you are feeling anger and unforgiveness:*

My Prince of Peace, there are times when I'm overtaken by anger. It can flare up at the smallest irritation—consuming my emotions and enflaming my reactions. I don't want to be ruled by anger . . . feeling on edge and out of control. Instead, I want the inner calm and self-control that your Spirit brings. Give me discernment to know when my anger is righteous and when it is not. Reign in my life so that anger won't lead me to sin.

When anger begins to arise, I want to remember you and call out for help. If there is some underlying factor behind my anger (like hurt, guilt, fear, or frustration), I ask you to reveal it and guide me as I seek to address the problem in a healthy way. When I'm mistreated and want to respond with retaliation and revenge, please restrain that urge. If I'm struggling to forgive, help me to keep asking you to fill me with your love and forgiveness toward those who have wronged me. If I need to take further steps to resolve conflict with someone, enable me to move forward in your grace, strength, and wisdom. Thank you that I can lean on you to defuse my anger and replace it with your peace.

## *When you are feeling guilt and shame:*

My Loving Father, these constant feelings of guilt and shame make me want to hide and shrink from your presence. Will I ever be free of this heavy self-condemnation? Will I ever feel forgiven and clean? How I yearn for acceptance! Jesus, remind me of the good news that your death and resurrection won for me the divine forgiveness and acceptance that I crave! Because of your victory, I can be assured of your warm, approving smile. Thank you for always wanting me to come to you—no matter my condition!

Please develop a pure, healthy conscience within me and empower me to walk in your ways. When I feel guilty because of sin, let it lead to confession and repentance. I ask you to liberate me from any lingering feelings of inappropriate guilt. If I'm assaulted by lies that define me as a bad person, bring to mind my new identity in you, Jesus. When shame persists in pointing its boney finger, I'm tempted to cover myself with "good" achievements . . . frantically trying to quiet the harsh accusations. Still, all my striving doesn't work. In these moments, help me look to you in childlike faith—trusting that your yoke is easy and your burden is light. This is possible because you perfectly fulfilled the righteous demands and expectations expressed in your law . . . and you did it on my behalf! May this reality provide relief and rest.

I trust that one day you will bring healing so that my feelings will align with your truth. But until then, steady me with deep confidence in knowing that you don't condemn me for these feelings. Thank you for understanding how hard and painful they are . . . and for the compassion in your eyes.

## *When you are feeling anxious and fearful:*

My Good Shepherd, I'm tied up in anxious knots and frozen with fear. I can't stop my mind from racing to the worst-case scenario all the time! My thoughts are constantly pulled in a direction that grips my heart with fear—which closes in around me like a prison. Please quiet my mind and enable me to take a deep breath. I want to live in the moment . . . not worrying about the past or fretting about the future. You are here with me right now. Help me to fix my eyes on you, your provision, and your protection.

Anxiety is such an exhausting burden. I'm frustrated because even if I place my cares in your hands, I often take them back again! I long to be free of these worries, but I'm not. Thank you for sympathizing with me and not judging. Though it is a wearying struggle, I know that you are fighting with and for me. I want to cooperate with you by filling my mind with your truth. Fortify me to faithfully spend time in your Word, in prayer, in worship, and with other believers. Even when I'm experiencing anxiety and fear, I know you are walking through this with me. Thank you!

## When you are feeling grief and loss:

My God of all comforts, I'm asking that you draw near to me now. I have suffered a loss that feels unbearable—as if part of me has been ripped away and stolen. Waves of emptiness, pain, and anxiety sweep over me at the oddest times. In those moments, I wonder how I can keep going . . . But I know that you can lift me out of the distress and fill my void with your fullness. Please show me if I need to seek additional help. If so, guide me to a good counselor. Jesus, thank you that you were willing to experience unspeakable loss for my sake. As a result, I have gained eternal life!

## When you're feeling broken:

Dear Lord, I'm regularly confronted with my brokenness. People have hurt me, and I've also embraced harmful lies about who I am. I recognize that even though my brokenness can be painful, you are using it to help me realize my weakness and my great need for you. In fact, you said that your power is made perfect in weakness.

I'm so grateful that I can be real with you about my brokenness and frailty, and you don't look down on me. What a comfort it is to know that you understand and will bring complete healing one day! You will create beauty from these ashes. When I feel broken beyond repair, please remind me of the good news that you have already made me new! I am part of your royal family! Since I bear your image, I have great dignity. I ask that you bring this thought to my troubled mind regularly and use it to foster healing. In Jesus' name I pray, Amen.

## When you don't understand the pain:

Lord God, depression is terrible, but I believe that you can use it to get my attention—like an emotional alarm system. I see that the pain can alert me to problems in my relationship with you and with the people I know and love. You can work through this darkness to shine a light on any dysfunctional patterns in the way that I think, act, or speak. May the heaviness prompt me to let go of destructive baggage from my past that weighs me down with resentment and fear. I want to move beyond self-condemnation and resignation to a place of lighthearted freedom and unshakable trust in you, my powerful Redeemer. Thank you for determining to use all this for your glory and my good.

***

Lord Jesus, please help me to believe that my suffering will produce greater maturity and yield something good that can benefit others. Even you had to endure suffering, but it achieved amazing things for the entire world! Though my life can feel meaningless, I know that I am connected to you, the source of all meaning! Enable me to fully embrace the hope I have in you. I also ask that you'll empower me to take steps in the right direction—accomplishing little activities that used to brighten my day; maybe they will eventually brighten my day again. Please protect me from believing the lie that my efforts don't matter. You are the One who fills each moment with significance—even when I can't see it. Remind me that my life is part of a bigger story that has a happy ending. I want to experience your love while finding purpose and enjoyment in a simple lifestyle. May these struggles cause me to revere you more deeply and obey you more fully.

## When God feels far away:

My Savior, thank you for being with me every step of this painful journey. You are no stranger to suffering, and the path of crucifixion that you walked through was more excruciating than I can fathom. You understand how I feel better than anyone else. Because of your suffering, I will eventually be free from my suffering. Not only that, but even now, you are working through my suffering to bring me future glory. Please generate in me an eternal mind-set that is focused on when there will be no more suffering. Help me to fix my thoughts on the glorious reality that awaits me in heaven. During the dark times, may this perspective provide the strength and perseverance I need to keep living in light of the truth.

*When overwhelmed by negative self-talk:*

Heavenly Father, sometimes my mind gets stuck in a negative rut—evaluating myself and my circumstances through the worst possible lens. Please help me to replace my defeating, demoralizing self-talk with uplifting promises found in the Bible. I recognize that it is vitally important for me to find nourishment in your life-giving Word instead of feeding on harmful accusations and speculations. Enable me to be intentional about remembering your promises—especially when I'm being pulled into old ways of thinking. As I consider your promises, keep me from a demanding, presumptuous attitude. May I hold each promise with humility—understanding that only you know when and how it will unfold in my life. I ask all this in Jesus' name, Amen.

*When you can't find hope:*

My Lord, this mental anguish has gone on for so long, and I am weary to the bone. I just want to give up—especially when I think that there is no chance of improvement. Please give me your strength . . . strength to endure . . . strength to keep trying to hope that there is hope. In this desolate season, I want to envision and anticipate a bright future where life is vibrant and joyful again. I know that pressing on through this trial with endurance can help me to grow. It will also make me more empathic and compassionate toward those who are suffering. Please enable me to wait on you and trust that you will renew my strength and give me hope.

*When you can't find rest:*

Lord God, initiator and keeper of the Sabbath, sometimes I'm driven to keep on working—whether out of a sense of the need to do more for God or to fulfill my own agenda. However, you have designed me, and you say that I need to implement a weekly rhythm of rest. Please help me to set aside work one day a week so that I can worship you with other believers and receive refreshment and renewal on a regular basis.

I want to enter into your rest both externally and internally . . . trusting in your finished work, Jesus. May my belief in you ease the pressures and rigors of daily life. I also want to spend time with you each day so that I can enjoy a life-giving oasis of rest more frequently. I believe this will infuse me with your strength . . . enabling me to better cope with the stress in my life.

I'm beginning to see that rest actually accomplishes a lot—and the benefits are profound! Thank you for the gift of rest!

## Lord, please heal:

Dear Lord, thank you for hearing my cries. I am so grateful for this incredible privilege of coming to you in prayer . . . and for how you can use it to bring healing. As I approach your throne of grace, please remind me of your tender compassion and your mighty power. When I earnestly plead for recovery, keep me from thinking that I know better than you—especially if your answer isn't what I want it to be. Enable me to surrender to your will and remain steadfast in my love for you. I know that the benefits and rewards of doing these two things will be very significant.

I want to persist in connecting with you through prayer. May this help me to keep my eyes on you—the source of all healing. You are able to do the impossible! I want to draw near to you in deep dependence, humility, and trust. Thank you that regardless of the degree of healing experienced in this life, I can know that you will bring complete healing in the next life. Jesus, because you were wounded and broken for us, we will be fully restored and made whole for all eternity! You are amazing!!!

# Selective Bibliography

THE SIX BOOKS THAT have asterisks (*) have been reviewed in detail by me because in some ways they are similar to my book. In this book, I have taken what I think is helpful from them and have ignored what I think is unhelpful.

*Bengtson, Michelle, PhD. *Hope Prevails: Insights from a Doctor's Personal Journey through Depression* (Grand Rapids: Revell, 2016). This book does a good job addressing many spiritual aspects of depression from the perspective of a previously depressed psychologist who has had many difficult life experiences and acknowledges many past misconceptions about what a truly godly Christian life looks like. Throughout her book, Bengtson shares very personal aspects of her struggles with and victories over depression; she is a wonderfully transparent Christian. She is also a helpful spiritual counselor, and she quotes Scripture often, usually but not always appropriately. Sometimes Bengtson spiritually challenges her readers in a way that, oddly enough, may be discouraging for clinically depressed people. Her recommendations of ways depressed people should think, feel, and act spiritually may be disheartening to clinically depressed people who have tried to apply her suggestions without improvement in their depressions. In fact, some clinically depressed people might feel like spiritual failures. A sense of spiritual failure certainly would have been the case for me if I had read some parts of her book while clinically depressed; I am so vulnerable and fragile at these times. The spiritual aspects addressed in my book focus mainly on spiritual aspects relevant to clinically depressed people, those who are more severely depressed, whereas Bengtson's book also addresses discouraged and mildly depressed people without differentiating them from more severely depressed people whom I think need a different approach. My book also addresses, in much more detail, the biomedical and some psychosocial aspects of depression than Bengtson's book. There are many other differences (mostly minor differences) in Bengtson's approach compared to mine in addressing the spiritual aspects of depression. For example, she places more weight on Satanic influence in depression than I would. I place more weight on the brokenness of human beings, without disregarding the fact that the devil, the father of lies and destroyer of people (John 8:44), will use our broken thoughts (often untrue thoughts) and feelings (often self-destructive feelings) against us. Though we have significant differences in our understanding of depression and in writing style, Bengtson has written a very good Christian book on the spiritual aspect of depression, and I recommend it to many of my Christian patients.

Carvalho, Andre, MD, and Roger MacIntyre. *Mental Health Disorders in Primary Care* (New York: Oxford University Press, 2017). As its title indicates, the book is for primary care physicians like me, helping physicians practice good medicine in treating mental illness.

Collins, Gary, PhD. *Christian Counseling: A Comprehensive Guide*, 3rd ed. (Nashville: Thomas Nelson, 2007). A classic practical guide to Christian counseling for behavioral health providers, especially clergy. I have used many of his insights in my book.

Dobson, Deborah, PhD, and Keith Dobson, PhD. *Evidence-Based Practice of Cognitive-Behavioral Therapy* (New York: Guilford, 2017). An excellent summary of the theory and practice of cognitive-behavioral therapy. Especially good for behavioral health providers but also helpful to healthcare professionals who really want to understand this important approach to counseling.

Gillihan, Seth, PhD. *Retrain Your Mind: Cognitive Behavioral Therapy in 7 Weeks* (Berkeley, CA: Althea, 2016). This is a very useful self-help workbook on managing depression and anxiety using CBT tools.

Greene-McCreight, Kathryn, PhD. *Darkness Is My Only Companion; A Christian Response to Mental Illness*, revised and expanded ed. (Grand Rapids: Brazos, 2015). Written by a Yale University chaplain and a very articulate author who has experienced severe bipolar disorder, this is, in my opinion, the best recent book on bipolar illness written by a Christian. Sharing her story of bipolar depression and mania and her resulting insights is a must read for Christians with bipolar disorder. The book is also written beautifully.

Greggo, Stephen, PsyD, and Timothy Sisemore, PhD. *Counseling and Christianity: Five Approaches* (Downers Grove, IL: IVP Academic, 2012). Helpful summaries of five Christian counseling approaches for behavioral health providers and interested healthcare providers and laypeople.

*Huang Harris, Jennifer, MD, Harold G. Koenig, MD, and John R. Peteet, MD. *Downcast: Biblical and Medical Hope for Depression* (Bristol, TN: Christian Medical and Dental Association, 2020). Written by three Christian psychiatrists, this book came out after I had sent the manuscript of my book to Cascade Press. This book had so much helpful information that my publisher allowed me to update my manuscript in light of this book. *Downcast* is similar to my book in many ways. It addresses biomedical, psychosocial, and Christian spiritual aspects of depression. Of course, there are some difference in content and perspective, but it is well worth reading by Christians who are depressed, as well as by family and friends, healthcare providers, counselors, and clergy. In my opinion it is one of the two best contemporary books on depression from a biomedical, psychosocial, and Christian spiritual perspective.

*Lovejoy, Gary, PhD, and Gregory Knopf, MD. *Light in the Darkness: Finding Hope in the Shadow of Depression* (Indianapolis: Wesleyan Publishing House, 2014). This book is similar to mine in many ways. It addresses the biomedical, psychosocial, and Christian spiritual aspects of depression. I believe it is a good book, but it doesn't differentiate clinically depressed people from discouraged or mildly depressed people. Many of the things Lovejoy, the psychologist, would suggest would not help clinically depressed people. Occasionally, but not often, Lovejoy suggests things that would be hurtful to some clinically depressed people. For example, Lovejoy does not consistently make it clear that the choices clinically depressed people need to make are extremely hard for them to make, and they often make bad choices because of their depression. When clinically depressed people do make good choices, they are often not rewarded in terms of healing from depression for weeks, months, or even years. I also think that depression is not first and foremost a God-given built-in alarm system. The idea of an alarm system is helpful, but I believe depression is primarily an aspect of our brokenness as human beings since the Edenic fall of humankind. Fortunately, God can use depression like an alarm system to help identify areas in the lives of depressed people that may have been neglected and need to be addressed. Knopf, the physician, and I differ about a number of aspects of the medical treatment of depression. Not least, he discourages many clinically depressed people from considering electroconvulsive therapy (ECT), which can be extremely helpful with very few side effects. It is especially helpful for treatment-resistant depression and depression associated with active suicidality or psychotic features. Despite these and other differences I think this book would be helpful to many depressed people, especially those less severely depressed. It is also a good book for Christian healers—healthcare providers, counselors, and clergy.

Mauer, Douglas, DO, MPH, Tyler Raymond, DO, MPH, and Bethany Davis, MD. "Depression: Screening and Diagnosis." *American Family Physician* (October 15, 2018) 508–15. Up-to-date information on screening and diagnosing depression for family medicine physicians and other primary care physicians.

McMinn, Mark, PhD, and Clark Campbell, PhD. *Integrative Psychotherapy: Toward a Comprehensive Christian Approach* (Downers Grove, IL: InterVarsity, 2007). A convincing and helpful integration of psychology and Christianity as it relates to psychotherapy and counseling. Especially good for behavioral health providers but also anyone trying to find a way to integrate important insights from secular psychology and biblical counseling.

Park, Lawrence, MD, and Carlos Zarate Jr., MD. "Depression in the Primary Care Setting." *New England Journal of Medicine* (February 7, 2019) 559–68. Up-to-date information on diagnosing and treating depression for primary care physicians, including family physicians.

*Piper, John, PhD. *When the Darkness Will Not Lift: Doing What We Can While We Wait for God and Joy* (Wheaton, IL: Crossway, 2006). John Piper wrote one of the most influential academic books in my thought life when I was studying in seminary, *The Justification of God*. Shortly thereafter he wrote one of the most influential books in my walk with God, *Desiring God*. Later, in 1992, Piper shared a very insightful reflection on the life of the recurrently severely depressed eighteenth-century poet and hymn lyricist, William Cowper, in "Insanity and Spiritual Songs in the Soul of a Saint." Piper's insights were helpful to me in writing about Cowper's life in my book. It grieves me, then, to recommend that depressed people not read *When Darkness Will Not Lift*. The book rightly draws attention to many rock-solid Reformed theological truths that I believe in, but it does not rightly apply them. For example, Piper rightly points out the importance of joy in the life of a Christian but then goes on to say, "Failing to rejoice in God when we are commanded to rejoice is sin." I strongly disagree with this. My book applies the Apostle Paul's encouragement to be joyful, cheerful, and glad much differently when dealing with clinically depressed people. But failing to rejoice when you have tried is definitely not a sin. At times clinically depressed people need to try to put themselves into situations where they may feel a little joy, cheerfulness, and gladness, but they should not feel guilty of sin when those feelings don't surface or last long. Sometimes when I am depressed, a hymn or spiritual song during worship will give me a partial, short-lived reprieve from depression. Piper also favorably quotes one of my favorite seventeenth-century Puritan pastors and writers, Richard Baxter: "Be sure that you live not idly, but in some constant business of a lawful calling, so far as you have bodily strength." Piper and I would agree with the first phrase in this sentence, but Piper would be on his own in neglecting the last phrase ("so far as you have bodily strength"). Clinically depressed people often don't have the motivation (their will is broken; they have no willpower) or energy (they experience exhausting mental and physical fatigue) to be "in some constant business of lawful calling." Piper calls the absence of joy, cheerfulness, and gladness "wrong feelings" and recommends preaching to yourself against them as though that will change wrong feelings into right feelings. He goes on to say, "But then exert your will and get up!" Getting up is just what many clinically depressed people want to do but can't, through no fault of their own. They have neither the motivation nor the energy. Finally, Piper points out that he is not a medical doctor but then quotes three people who clearly have a strong bias against the use of medication in the treatment of depression, none of whom are physicians. I don't understand why some people, like Piper, are so worried about the negative effects of antidepressants on our spiritual lives when they also believe that these medications are no better than placebos. In my book, we examine these purported negative effects of antidepressants and their placebo effects. There are some helpful things in Piper's book, but there are too many potentially hurtful things to recommend it to clinically depressed people or those who care about them. In fact, I recommend against reading Piper's book if you are clinically depressed. The broken mind of a clinically depressed person is a fragile thing that can be easily completely shattered by well-meaning but misguided people.

Preston, John, PsyD, and James Johnson, MD. *Clinical Psychopharmacology Made Ridiculously Simple*, 9th ed. (Miami, FL: MedMaster, 2019). A practical guide for both healthcare professionals and behavioral health providers to readily understand the most important aspects of the medical treatment of mental illness.

Rakel, Robert, MD, and David Rakel, MD, eds. *Textbook of Family Medicine*, 9th ed. (Philadelphia: Elsevier Saunders, 2016). A classic textbook for family medicine physicians that includes an important chapter on the diagnosis and medical treatment of depression and anxiety together.

Sadock, Benjamin, MD, Virginia Sadock, MD, and Pedro Ruiz, MD. *Concise Textbook of Clinical Psychiatry*, 11th ed. (Philadelphia: Wolters Kluwer, 2017). Mainly a book for psychiatrists and other healthcare providers.

Schneider, Robert K., MD, and James L. Levenson, MD. *Psychiatry Essentials for Primary Care* (Philadelphia: American College of Physicians, 2008). Still a good book on diagnosing and treating mental illness for primary care physicians including family medicine physicians.

Shapero, Benjamin, PhD. *The Massachusetts General Hospital Guide to Depression: New Treatment Insights and Options* (New York: Humana, 2019). For healthcare professionals and behavioral health specialists who want an in-depth discussion of many hot topics in the treatment of depression.

Weissman, Myrna, PhD, John Markowitz, MD, and Gerald Klerman, MD. *The Guide to Interpersonal Psychotherapy*, rev. and expanded ed. (New York: Oxford University Press, 2018). An excellent summary of interpersonal psychotherapy. Especially good for behavioral health providers but also helpful to healthcare professionals who really want to understand this important approach to counseling.

*Welch, Edward. *Depression: Looking Up from the Stubborn Darkness* (Greensboro, NC: New Growth, 2011). Welch's book focuses on the spiritual aspect of depression from a consistently biblical point of view. There is much wisdom his book, but as with Piper, there are also many hurtful things. He and Piper believe that sharing things that are hurtful to depressed people is justified. The problem, in part, is that both Welch and Piper fail to recognize that biblical truths need to be applied differently to those who are discouraged or mildly depressed from those who are moderately to severely depressed. Another part of the problem may be that neither Welch nor Piper are likely to have experienced a moderate to severe depression. I don't know this for a fact, but they just don't seem to get it. While I disagree with some of Welch's counseling approaches, I especially disagree with his assessment of the medical aspects of depression. His mistakes are understandable since he is a trained counselor, not a physician. I don't think Welch really understands how many people have been relieved from many of the very painful aspects of depression with medication alone. I always counsel patients to get counseling; depression is a life-changing experience that needs to be used to the best advantage in depressed people's growth as Christians. But many of my patients treated with medication alone who have neither the inclination nor the time nor the money for counseling have been completely relieved from all the symptoms of depression. They experience God-given joy, renewed energy, peaceful nights, greater motivation, and many other good things without biblical counseling. Medications alone often *do* relieve "the guilt, fear, self-loathing, and other distinctly spiritual symptoms" that Welch says medications don't help. This is not to say that counseling should be dismissed. But counselors like Welch do not understand the power of medication, one of God's means of common grace for healing clinically depressed people. I would recommend against reading Welch's book.

*Winter, Richard, MD. *When Life Goes Dark: Finding Hope in the Midst of Depression*. (Downers Grove, IL: InterVarsity, 2012). This book is very well written and researched by a British Christian psychiatrist and orthodox American seminary professor. It is, in my opinion, one of the two best contemporary books on depression from a Christian perspective of the biomedical, psychosocial, and spiritual aspects of depression. Dr. Winter's book is thorough in terms of its content and documentation of sources. This is of great benefit to Christian healthcare providers, counselors, and clergy, but it is too detailed for most clinically depressed people and their family and friends to read. Dr. Winter's footprints are all over my book. His section on the biomedical aspects of depression is helpful but mine is more practical for clinically depressed patients than his. I especially turn to Dr. Winter's judgment on issues related to in-depth Christian counseling of depressed people. In the context of my practice of family medicine, I only do brief counseling though many of my depressed patients need more in-depth counseling. Dr. Winter is also a fine biblical interpreter and practical theologian, but I think my skills as a biblical interpreter and practical theologian are equal to his.

Yatham, Lakshmi, et al. "Canadian Network for Mood and Anxiety Treatments and International Society for Bipolar Disorders: 2018 Guidelines for the Management of Patients with Bipolar Disorder." *Bipolar Disorders: An International Journal of Psychiatry and Neuroscience* (March 14, 2018) 97–170. Mainly for psychiatrists but helpful to primary care physicians, including family medicine physicians, who want more in-depth knowledge of bipolar disorder treatments.

# Author's Professional Training and Experience

I HAVE BEEN A family physician for more than forty-three years. I trained as a medical student at the University of Michigan Medical School, then as a family medicine resident at the Medical University of South Carolina. In my second year of private medical practice, I had a strong desire to learn more about the Bible. I took a course on the Hebrew language at Andrews University, in Berrien Springs, Michigan, where I was practicing. I loved it and knew that I would love other seminary courses as well. For six years, I practiced family medicine part time and studied part time at Gordon-Conwell Theological Seminary, earning a Master of Arts in Theological Studies. Soon after graduating from seminary, I helped start Beverly Hospital Family Medicine Residency in the Boston area. The first year in the residency I completed a Fellowship in Primary Care Faculty Development at Michigan State University. Two years later, I became the founding director of the Shenandoah Valley Family Medicine Residency in Winchester and Front Royal, Virginia. After seven years, I went into private medical practice, where I have been ever since. I continue to have an appointment as Associate Clinical Professor of Family Medicine at Virginia Commonwealth University School of Medicine. In 2008, I received the Teacher of the Year Award from the Virginia Academy of Family Physicians. For the last four years I have been regularly lecturing to lay and medical audiences on depression and other mental illnesses in the United States and Kenya.